curiot

Clwyd

A Second Photographic Album of

Oddities from Northeast Wales

To Alan

TEXT, GRAPHICS AND PUBLICATION BY

©1996

GORDON EMERY

27 GLADSTONE ROAD, CHESTER CHI 4BZ

PHOTOGRAPHS BY

©1996

MIKE PENNEY

LRPS

mike Penney

No part of this book may be reproduced in any form or by
any means without the permission of the copyright owner.

Printed by **MASONS DESIGN & PRINT** 01244 674433

Printed on Savannah Natural Matt,
produced from at least 60% bagasse – a waste product of the sugar cane process.

credits

Thanks to all the people who have informed me of oddities, allowed me access to their property, and given me information. In particular I would like to thank the staff of Clwyd libraries and record offices (now Flintshire and Denbighshire once more) for their help, Jim Bentley for information and sketches on the slate mines at Glyndyfrdwy, Leslie White at Berse Drelincourt, Tom Smith for his guided tour of Althrey Hall, and Bill Slater for his explanation of Minera Lead Mines.

John Morgan spent many hours producing hand prints of all the photographs. It is unfortunate that even though all the photos were scanned before printing, it is still difficult to reproduce the depth of the originals in a printed book. Hand prints of all the photographs from both volumes of Curious Clwyd are available in any size. Individual quotes are available from the author or Storm Photography, 30 Tregele Close, Blacon, Chester.

contents

cover

FRONT

    top: 'Sun' emblem from Llanerchrugog Hall Lodge, Rhosllanerchrugog

also see page 135

    bottom: The author's son sitting on a 300 kilo Lego brick

see page 140

REAR

    top left: The pump at Bretton Lane, Broughton

see also CC1 p 118

    bottom left: Dyserth Waterfall

see page 46

    top right: Owain Glyndŵr portrayed on the hotel of the same name at Corwen

    bottom centre: The Jesus statue at the RC Primary School at Holywell was brought from Italy by ship, train and horse-drawn waggon in the 1920s. The school is about to be demolished.

see also page 43 and CC1 p 114

diagonal: butterflies - orange tip (top) Anthocaris cardamines can be found in damp meadows with garlic mustard and cuckoo flower.
small tortoiseshell (bottom) Aglais urticae; as the Latin name suggests, this butterfly is found on nettle.
swallowtail (centre) Papilio machaon; this butterfly is restricted to mainland Europe and the English fens. The only ones normally seen in Northeast Wales are those produced by The Original Butterfly Man Craft Workshops in Glyndyfrdwy where all these came from.

see page 134

curiouser...

A few of my mistakes have come to light since the first Curious Clwyd was published. I have also been notified, by interested readers, of several more oddities in the area.

Immediately after publication I visited Denbigh and realised, to my shame, that I had forgotten the stocks in the town centre and written (CC1 p95) that the Llangwyfan stocks were "the only remaining stocks in the county". I can only apologise. Furthermore I was informed, by a Mr Morgan of Milton Keynes, that the three Canadian soldiers killed in the Kinmel mutiny (CC1 p59) were not buried in the churchyard at Bodelwyddan. (According to research by a visitor, Mr J C Kent of Toronto, all the soldiers there died of disease.) The church at Buckley is dedicated to St Mark, not St Mary. The other baptistry is at Lower Soughton not Soughton Hall as I stated.

Beeboles in the 18th century barn at Pen-y-wern.

I was also informed where items similar to those in the book were found in other areas, eg the box pews at Bronington and Llangar. Howell Edwards reminded me about the pack-horse bridge at Penycae, and Dr Forbes wrote to tell me of another set of beeboles - in his barn. He was aware of their nature but had not known there was a national register to record those remaining. Mr Asher of Ruabon gave me the grid reference of the Wynnstay icehouse: it is only a short distance from the memorial column in this book. Paul Parry told me of two more icehouses, at Gyrn Castle, Llanasa, and at Talacre Abbey where there may be another dovecote. I have found a few more dovecotes and have been shown a converted one by Ken Farrell: The Pigeonaire in Penley (see page 66).

Elizabeth, the doll in the window at Coedpoeth (CC1 p9) can no longer be found there. Her owner suffered ill-health

5

and had to move to Acrefair. A farewell story was printed in the local newspaper.

I had failed to mention to readers of my first book of oddities that all the items were linked by place, shape or pun. Some readers noticed that a few were connected, whilst others thought the listing rather random. Now you know. Linking items again, I have started where I left off, with Mr McGregor's house in Beatrix Potter's book. The last item, Lego, as a children's toy links with the doll at the start of the first book. There will not be another volume of Curious Clwyd, although I would still like to hear of other icehouses and dovecotes.

In my last introduction I mentioned several books which give comprehensive information about the former county. Now I recommend two more:
'The RSPB Book of Bird watching in Clwyd' gives a map and spotters' guide to the area.
'Flora of Flintshire' was rather behind its time when it claimed to be "the flowering plants and ferns of a North Wales county" (Flintshire had ceased to exist 20 years before) but now that the new counties have been created, and there is once again a Flintshire, this time without its detatchment* in the Maelor, one wonders where the author, Goronwy Wynne, received his advance information. Needless to say, the book is an interesting and informative record of plantlife in Northeast Wales and includes some natural curiosities. One of these, the milk thistle, I found in profusion below St Beuno's Cave (page 78) and yet only a few sites have been recorded in Clwyd.

*Part of old Flintshire to the south of Wrexham was separated from the main county.

John Seller's 1694 map of Flintshire (based on Speed's 16th century map).

...and curiouser

Clwyd, as a county, has become extinct. This second volume is dedicated to its short life (born 1974 - died 1996). Historians will, no doubt, argue as to whether the reorganisation of Wales into unitary authorities was for the purpose of simplifying services and cutting costs, or reducing the political power of the big six Welsh counties (now devolved into over 20 smaller ones). On one hand Clwyd County Council had made significant advances with its own Archaeology Service, Conservation Officer and Ecology Officer; whilst its legal system was all but an appalling

bureaucracy where it took 2 years to get a double yellow line on a road, and up to 11 years to get a footpath diverted.

Culturally there has been a loss, if only in Welsh place names. The county, borough and district names which included Clwyd, Maelor, Alyn, Delyn and Rhuddlan as well as Glyndŵr have been replaced by the former English names of Flintshire, Denbighshire and Wrexham (from Wristlesham - Saxon) but with different boundaries guaranteed to confuse historians. (The formation of Clwyd had already confused the publishers of Hubbard's 'Buildings of Wales, Clwyd'. The map in his book shows the boundary of Clwyd to the west of Betws-y-coed!)

Unfortunately I was unable to photograph one curiosity in Clwyd ...

timewarp
When a fairly down-to-earth employee from British Aerospace visited his friend's old house in Hope, in due course he asked to use the toilet and was told that it was upstairs. Accordingly he climbed the stairs and, upon reaching the first floor, could not find a toilet but a girl in old-fashioned dress passed in front of him. Feeling rather bewildered he went downstairs to ask again where the toilet was, but on arrival found his friend very agitated. "Where have you been?" asked his friend. "You've been gone an hour. I've looked all over the house for you."

With a 20-25% raise in council tax rates many residents now wish they were in a timewarp and Clwyd still existed.

"THEY watched him go into his house.
And then they crept up to the window to listen."
' From The Tale of the Flopsy Bunnies' by Beatrix Potter

beatrix potter's garden

DENBIGH   SJ034654

The garden is open to the public via Countryworld on the Pentrefoelas Road.

Mentioning Beatrix Potter conjures visions of Peter Rabbit and the English Lake District. It was in the Lakes that she wrote many of her later animal tales. As Mrs Heelis she lived the latter half of her life there, and beque large estate, bought with the proceeds of her books, to the National Trust.

Earlier, as the unmarried daughter of the Potter family, her inspiration was drawn from her pets in the family's London town house and from places where she stayed on long summer holidays. One of these was Gwaynynog (now Gwaenynog) which belonged to her uncle John Burton, who, like her father, had inherited a large fortune made in the cotton industry.

The walled garden at Gwaenynog still has visible signs of 'The Tale of the Flopsy Bunnies': the 'ditch' (actually a ha-ha to stop stock animals entering) outside the garden where Mr McGregor threw his rubbish, the view across the field to the rear gate, and 'Mr McGregor's house'.

In summer a riot of flowers fills the senses, while the new apple trees planted by the current owner have been espaliered to match Beatrix Potter's description in her diaries.

At one end of the garden there survives a set of tollgate posts formerly situated on the main road. (See also CC1 p18.)

"WHILE he was gone, Mrs Flopsy Bunny (who had remained at home) came across the field."

Overleaf: 'Mr McGregor's house'

The Sphinx

sphinx

LEESWOOD

Access is by road

SJ250616

Is it human or animal? Neither: this is a representation of the Sphinx of Greek mythology. One appears on each stone plinth at the sides of the White Gates at Leeswood (see CC1 p125). Most people think of the Great Sphinx in Egypt but that is said to be a statue of the 4th dynasty Egyptian King Khaf-Ra with the body of a lion.

Statues of sphinxes lined the approach to the Egyptian city of Thebes and possibly gave rise to the Greek legend. The Sphinx, a monster with a woman's head and breasts, a lion's body, an eagle's wings and a serpent's tail, lay in wait for travellers outside the Greek city of Thebes. Every person who tried to pass was asked a riddle, "What has four feet in the morning, two feet at noon and three feet in the evening, with only one voice?" Anyone who failed to answer correctly was strangled and devoured. Oedipus answered the riddle correctly, whereupon the Sphinx killed itself. The thankful Thebians then made Oedipus king.

The answer to the riddle is a human who first crawls, then walks, then uses a walking stick in old age.

magpie cottage

HANMER   SJ455396

The cottage, a private residence, can be seen opposite the mere, next to the village post office.

Did magpies nest in this thatch? Probably not, as this species of bird does not normally use straw or reed to make its nests. Formerly just known as 'The Cottage' it was built in the 16th century with a wooden frame infilled with wattle and daub: interwoven twigs, usually hazel or briar, plastered with a mixture of clay, lime, dung and sometimes straw. The name Magpie comes from its black and white facade.

Magpie Cottage

dovecote

ERBISTOCK   SJ355403

At the time of writing this could be seen at Veg-to-Table, an organic garden beside the road in the village.

This pseudo-Georgian dovecote, probably originally erected at Horsley Hall in Marford during the early 20th century, appeared in the grounds of Veg-to-Table during 1994. No planning permission had been given to the owner, Simon Dyson-Wingett, a local auctioneer. He claims that he had not realised that he was moving a listed building, and rebuilt the top in a different style. In July 1995 listed building consent was refused. Later, in October, a planning application (in retrospect) was also turned down. The building may have to be returned to its original location.

Horsley Hall was demolished in 1963; its stables are in ruins; the garden is overgrown and a screen wall (believed to have come from a London house inhabited by Peter the Great in 1697) collapsed in 1978. While listed building protection and planning consent are necessary, in this instance one wonders if it might be better to restore this unusual piece of architecture, next to the pseudo-Georgian house in Erbistock where it can be seen by the public.

The rebuilt dovecote

The former roof with dove doors.

dovecote

GWESPYR   SJ128825

Access by written permission from the owner at Bryn Morfa, Tan y lan.

Look up to your right just beyond the Talacre roundabout as you travel the coast road from Prestatyn to Flint. The 17th century dovecote was in a ruinous state when the house was built adjacent to it. At one time it would have had entrances for the doves above the alighting ledge. The owner repaired the nesting boxes inside and fitted a new roof. The building is now used as a shed, the nesting boxes as handy cubby-holes.

There is no great house nearby although the area, once known as Werdd Log, may have been an ancient fortified site. Henry Tudor, later Henry VII, is said

Outside
the
dovecote

to have escaped from his pursuers at this spot where, disguised as a peasant with a faggot (bundle of sticks) over his shoulder, he made his way down to a fisherman on the coast and ultimately sailed to Brittany.

At that time the sea wall had not been constructed (this was built in George III's reign) and the flat lands regularly flooded. Old maps show Offa's Dyke coming to the nearby headland which was named 'Point Offa'. With the second syllable pronounced in a Welsh accent it is easy to see why the new headland became known as 'Point of Air'. Later on, another misinterpretation of the name was made by the owners of the coal mine who named it 'Point of Ayr'. The last coal from here, the last coal mine in North Wales, was brought up on 23rd August 1996.

Inside the dovecote

Game Larder

Inside the larder

game larder
SOUGHTON

SJ247674

Soughton Hall is a hotel open for functions.

The Chester architect John Douglas may have designed this unusual octagonal game larder. It was built in 1872 at the rear of Soughton Hall (see page 125).

pinfold
CAERWYS

The pinfold stands beside the road.

Before the Inclosure Acts in the 18th century, land was open with strips or 'quillets' (a word unlisted in the dictionary but regularly used in documents and maps from this area) rented out by the local Lord of the Manor. Animals were grazed upon the common, much of which still exists on Halkyn Mountain where, to this day, over 200 commoners have rights to graze sheep. When the animals wandered from the common to the arable land they would be rounded up by the pinder (a name which has survived as a surname) and deposited in the pinfold until the owner came to claim them. This high-walled pinfold is still intact at Caerwys while the low remaining walls of another surround the war memorial at Caergwrle. The tithe map (mid-19th century) shows a pinfold on the main road at Penley.

Caerwys Pinfold

One of the whalebones at Whalebone Farm.

whale bones

WILLINGTON   SJ439434

Access is only by written permission from
Whalebone Farm.

Last century when a farmer in Willington
told his mate, a whaler, to bring him back
one of the giant bones he talked about,
the farmer could have been joking. One
wonders how the two jawbones of a whale
were transported home, as even in their
dried condition it takes two people to
lift each one. The property was renamed
Whalebone Farm. By the porch hangs a
ship's bell but that is another story.

Mounting steps

mounting steps & dog tongs

LLANYNYS   SJ103627

The mounting steps are outside the church gates. The dog tongs are inside the
church. A keyholder's address is posted in the porch.

These steps date from the days when Llanynys Church was attended by
parishioners who travelled on horseback or in carriages. Nowadays they make
a useful bike rest. On the church door
can be seen an example of 16th century
graffiti (see page 145). Inside the building,
in addition to the 15th century wall painting
(page 133) and the sepulchral stone (page 44)
there is an unusual tool. The walk, or ride,
to church was also an opportunity to exercise
the dog, but rather than tie the animal
outside it was allowed in. This would
frequently result in unsocial behaviour.
The church warden would use the dog tongs
to separate the beasts and evict one or
more from the premises.

Dog tongs

19

Knife rests

Fox & stile

WREXHAM   SJ316508

At present these can only be viewed by written permission from the owners,
Mr & Mrs White at Berse Drelincourt.

You will not find either of these on a public footpath. Both are silver-plated, and
the stile is approximately 8cm long by 6cm tall. Both are early 20th century English
knife rests. They are part of a unique collection in the possession of Mr and Mrs
White whose interest in the subject has led them to travel to antique shops
and auctions here and abroad.

With tablecloths becoming fashionable in the 17th century, the aristocracy then had
to find a way to keep cutlery from spoiling it. Silver was the first choice.
However, by Victorian times, cutlery rests, and later just carving set rests, were
prolific, which led to the use of other materials and a host of different styles.
Although rarely seen at table settings nowadays, cutlery rests are still used on
the Continent while new sets can be bought in York or London.

Cutlery rests

1 Perspex, with small red roses within, mid-C20th
2 fairly common 4 loop pattern, late C19th
3 lead glass (cut glass look), early C20th
4 glass, early C20th
5 standard pattern hexagonal glass, C20th
6 sawbench, silver plate, English, C20th
7 standard diagonal cross, C20th
8 3 loop twisted bar, early C20th
9 pair of lions, silver plate, German 1910
10 blue and white ceramic pottery, English by Rogers (staffs?) 1800-1820
11 lead glass fish with red eyes, 1930s
12 silver plate vine leaves with grapes, late C19th
13 silver plate (EPNS) intertwining dolphins, English, C20th

Mr & Mrs White would be interested in seeing other knife rests or collections.

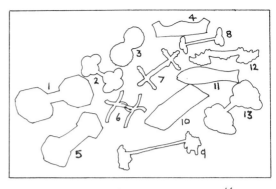

Key

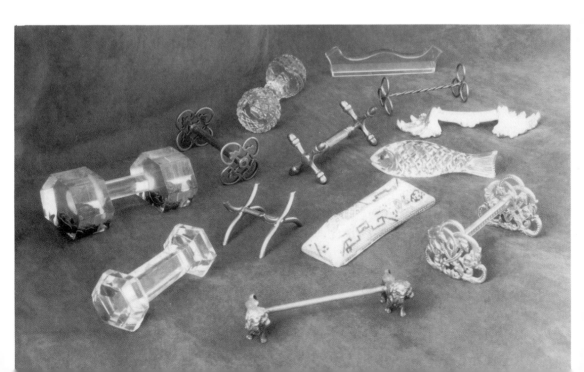

slab stile

YSCEIFIOG   SJ151715

A public path goes through the churchyard.

This stile at the rear of Ysceifiog Church should last longer than its wooden equivalents. A close inspection of the slab reveals that it is a reused gravestone. The path, like many others, leads from the surrounding hamlets to the village and its church.

Slab stile

Other examples of the footpath network leading to the churches at the village centres can be found in Gresford, Hanmer and Worthenbury.

tramline stile

PANTYMWYN   SJ196650

The stile is beside the road.

Pantymwyn translates as hollow-of-mines, and the reuse of a tramway rail as the top bar of this stile is one reminder of the mining that took place on Mold Mountain in the last century. (See also page 49.)

Tramline stile

new stiles for old

PENLEY   SJ429393

This footpath leads from the A539 at Stryt Lydan towards Tarts Hill.

Old and new stiles

An old oak stile dated 1912, and originally erected by the Kenyons of Gredington, has now been moved to become part of the fence alongside a new preservative -treated pine stile.* The posts on the oak stile had rotted at ground level but otherwise the wood is harder than it would have been when it was built 83 years before the new one.

The design of stiles by the Gredington Estate is similar to that of the Bryn-y-pys Estate in Overton. During the early part of the 20th century tenants at Overton were given new oak stiles to erect on public paths across their land. Account books, now at the Record Office in Hawarden, show many deliveries, including the following: 20th March 1904 Knolton 2 stiles, 23rd November 1904 Blackwood 1 stile, 5th June 1905 Carregofranc 1 stile, 10th June 1905 Rhewl 1 stile.

Tenancy agreements show that as well as cutting thistles in July, tenants had to cut hedges on public roads in June and October, and keep stiles in good repair.

Gates too were supplied by the estate. On 4th November 1905 a quote was given to the estate office for twelve 9ft gates in oak @ 12/9d each or twenty @ 12/6d each. This bargain discount of about 6% was obviously too good to miss, for scrawled across the quotation in red ink is the instruction, 'Get 20'. At least two of these gates, dated 1905, can still be found on local farms in the area.

* The new stile is one of over a thousand built or repaired in the Wrexham area by the author.

Above : The path starts at the door of St Beuno's College
Right : A gate on the path
Below : St Mary's Church (rock chapel)

private public path

TREMEIRCHION   SJ 081739

There is no public access to this public path!

The Definitive Map of Public Rights of Way for the County of Clwyd, available for inspection with the new unitary authorities, clearly shows a public path leading from the back door of St Beuno's College to the foot of a small hill, Garreg Fawr. Despite being inaccessible to the public, the path is well used, for at the top of the hill is Our Lady of Sorrows, also known as Rock Chapel. Surrounded by trees it was built in 1868 and designed by a student at the Jesuit college.

Another path with no access to it leaves a private track on the Gwrych Castle Estate in Abergele and goes to a well.

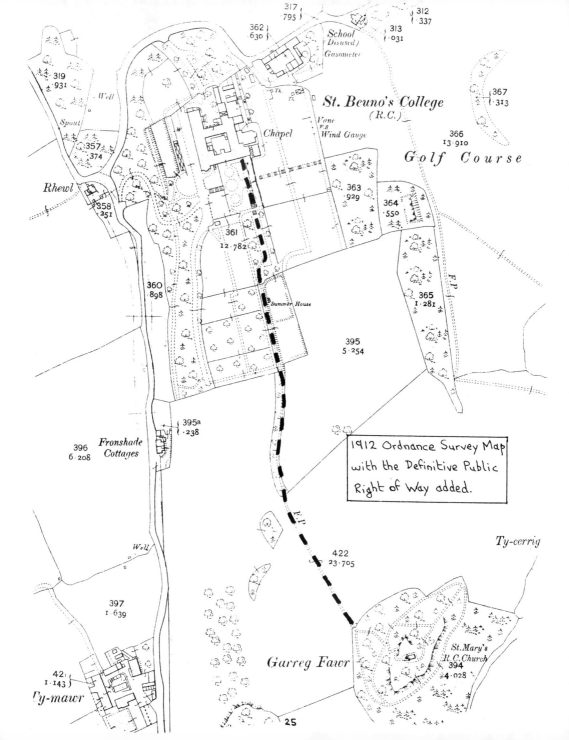

317
795

312
·337

362
·630

School
(Disused)
Gasometer

313
·031

319
931

Well

367
·3¹³

Spout

St. Beuno's College
(R.C.)

Chapel

Vane
F.S.
Wind Gauge

366
13·910

Golf   Course

357
374

Rhewl

363
·929

358
·251

364
·550

361
12·782

F.P.

360
·898

Summer House

365
1·281

395
5·254

395a
·238

1912 Ordnance Survey Map
with the Definitive Public
Right of Way added.

396
6·208

Fronshade
Cottages

Ty-cerrig

Well

F.P.

422
23·705

397
1·639

Garreg Fawr

St.Mary's
R.C.Church
394
4·028

42¹
1·143

Ty-mawr

25

Erbistock Mill has an inscribed date of 1602

no through bridleway

OVERTON   SJ 358422

The bridleway starts from the A539 Overton-Wrexham road.

If you follow the Overton bridleway from the A539 it leads to the bank of the River Dee at Erbistock weir. This was an old ford and may have been used before the nearby road bridge was built. However, the two tracks on the other side of the river have been lost to riders. One, leading almost to the water's edge, has 'Strictly Private' signs on it. In 1952, when the parish councils of Overton and Erbistock claimed rights-of-way for the definitive map, they seem to have neglected to check that their neighbouring parish council had recorded the continuation of the bridleways.

Farther upstream, beside the Boat Inn, an Erbistock bridleway is recorded to the parish boundary in the centre of the Dee, but Overton Parish Council did not claim their side. This omission is perhaps more surprising as the landowner states that the ford here was used in the 1940s by American soldiers with horses.

There are records of a guarded river crossing (either by the weir, at the bridge, or both) in 1643 during the Civil War. In 1651 it was estimated that £400 was needed to repair the bridge and by 1666 a new bridge had been constructed. The present road bridge dates from 1816.

horseshoe falls

LLANTYSILIO   SJ 196433

The falls can be reached by following the canal westwards from Llangollen,
Chain Bridge or Berwyn Station.

Thomas Telford built this almost semi-circular weir across the River Dee
to channel water into the Llangollen Arm of the Ellesmere Canal (now
known as the Llangollen Canal). The weir spans approximately 140 metres
and comprises square faced stones just over 3 metres high, clipped together
with cast-iron cappings nearly 3 metres long. The canal from the Dee
to Pontcysyllte was, in fact, only built as a navigable feeder for the
Ellesmere Canal. Only half-laden boats could travel west of Llangollen. In 1947
a valve house was erected at the inlet to comply with regulations for
measuring the flow of water. Up to 55 million litres a day flow through it.

Horseshoe Falls

horse gin

BERSHAM   SJ311491

Bersham Heritage Centre is open to the public.

A one-horsepower engine, without the horse, stands outside Bersham Heritage Centre. Nearby, at Bersham Ironworks, the Octagonal Building – used as a cannon foundry by John Wilkinson – may be sited on the circular foundation of a building that once housed a horse gin. The building for a horse gin can be found at Plas-yn-y-pentre in Trevor, whilst a Coed Gerynant (horse gin wood) stands about a mile from Llandrillo.

Reconstructed Horse Gin

Octagonal Building

Although water mills were prevalent in the Welsh valleys, a drought would create a temporary loss of power. Horse gins would have been more reliable (as long as a good supply of carrots was available).

The history of 'Iron-mad' John Wilkinson can be seen at the Bersham exhibitions. Wilkinson produced the first iron boat to prove his theories. He even built an iron pulpit, as well as iron sand trays for school pupils to practise writing with an iron stylus, to save paper.

Wilkinson also made a fortune 'printing his own money'. After the Royal Mint stopped making copper coins in 1754, partly because of the copper shortage and the expense of running their hand presses, the country was short of loose change. This resulted in the increasing use of trade tokens and the minting of small coins by several industrialists who had a large payroll. Wilkinson was given a licence to produce money, making nearly 40% profit after paying the Crown and buying the materials. From 1787 to 1798 he produced copper pennies which could be cashed in at his various works at Bradley Willey, Snedshill and Bersham, and later at Liverpool and London. The coins were struck with his own face on one side cheekily resembling King George III. As a result he was sarcastically referred to as 'The Iron Monarch'. He also produced silver coins, tokens in leather and guinea (£1/1s/0d) notes.

The 'Iron Monarch' on his copper penny of 1787 (enlarged - courtesy of K. Farrell)

The Racecourse

racecourse

HOLYWELL   SJ152756

A public bridleway can be followed around part of the course.

In 1767 the Mostyn Estate purchased land for about £200 to create a running track. When the first meeting of the Holywell Hunt took place on Thursday 9th November 1769, the horses were 'rode by Gentlemen'. Later they were 'rode by Jockeys'.

By the mid-18th century the Duke of Westminster was regularly attending the Holywell Hunt, and taking a complete hotel in the town for his accommodation. One year the duke arrived to find a commercial traveller had taken a room in the hotel. The commoner was asked to leave the hotel but stuck to his rights and refused, making the duke so angry that he never returned. Instead he bought a house nearby which became 'Halkyn Castle'.

The two mile and one furlong racecourse at Holywell closed in the mid-1950s.

HOLYWELL HUNT.

Printed (by Permission of the Gentlemen of the Hunt). by E. Carnes, Holywell.

THURSDAY October 18, 1804.

A SWEEPSTAKES

OF FIVE GUINEAS EACH. P. P.

For half bred Horses, the beft of three one mile heats, to be rode by Jockeys, five years old to carry 11ft. 11lb. six years old 12ft. 4lb. and aged 12ft. 6lb.

T. Moftyn Edwards, Esq's gr. m. Cinderella,
    6 Years old, Gamble, Green and Red.

S. W. Cotton, Esq. br. g. Stick Pig, six years old
    Rider unknown.

Sir T. Moftyn, Bart. did not name.

Bell Lloyd, Esq. did not name.

E Lloyd Lloyd. Esq. did not name,

Sir E Pryce Lloyd, did not name.

H. E. Boates, Esq. did not name.

J. M. Moftvn, Esq. did not name.

Owen M. Wynne, Esq. did not name.

T. Pennant, Esq. did not name.

P. Lloyd Fletcher, Esq. did not name.

T. Cholmondeley, Esq. did not name.

  Also A BAG RACE and SMOCK RACE
from the Diftance Chair to the Stand, the winner
of each to have *Five Guineas, and the second of each*
One Guinea.

The four dogs

four dogs

ACTON

SJ 336515

View from the Chester Road.

Ready for the off! Four upright greyhounds proudly adorn the Greek Doric screen at the formal entrance to Acton Park.

In 1620 most of Acton belonged to John Jeffreys. The large hall was taxed for 11 hearths under an early forerunner to our Council Tax system in 1670, the same year that saw the birth of a fifth son to John Jeffreys the younger; the son was destined to become the infamous 'Hanging Judge' – Lord Chancellor, Lord Jeffreys of Wem (see CCI p 177).

Ellis Yonge of Bryn Iorcyn, Hope bought the estate for £4784 in 1674; in 1787 it was sold by his executors to Sir Foster Cunliffe of Saighton in Cheshire. Only a few years later the new Chester to Wrexham turnpike road altered his boundaries.

The new parkland around the hall was enclosed and, to keep up with Georgian fashion, a new driveway to the hall was built. Thomas Harrison, a famous architect from Chester, who designed the Grosvenor Bridge, Chester Castle and the Moel Famau Jubilee Tower, drew up plans for the entrance screen. The crest of the Cunliffe Baronetcy included greyhound, seajant, argent, collared sable; and to represent this four upright (seajant) greyhounds were carved from wood in the Edwards' joiners shop in Lavister and painted silver (argent) with black collars.

The breakup of the estate and the sale of the hall and parkland to Wrexham District Council saw the screen fall into disrepair. One dog disappeared in 1944, coincidentally when the American army left the area; another was dumped in a hedge half-a-mile away during 1964. The hall was demolished during 1956. However the Civic Society pressed councillors to keep the screen, and although suggestions that it should be moved were made, common sense and the prohibitive transportation cost kept it in its original position, albeit with a new housing estate behind it.

When Wrexham Lager Brewery built a pub adjacent to the entrance, a competition was held for its name. 'The Judge Jeffreys' was suggested but 'The Four Dogs' was chosen. This gave impetus to the screen's restoration. Joss Buncher and Graham Evans of Wrexham Art College, funded by Wrexham Lager, produced four glass fibre and concrete greyhounds based on one of the original wooden carvings. In April 1982 the restored screen, cleaned of graffiti, was formally opened.

Offices of Wrexham Lager - a British first for lager.

a thirst for lager

WREXHAM   SJ 329505

The brewery is prominent in Wrexham.

"I enclose herewith one of your labels which was taken off a bottle found in the grounds of Gordon's Palace at Khartoum on September 3rd 1898. I send it as a matter of curiosity, just to let you know how far your famous Wrexham Lager Beer can be had."

This letter was sent from Sudan by a Sergeant Major James Gourley of the British forces under Kitchener who had relieved Khartoum and expelled the Mahdi - a little too late for General Gordon and the bottle of lager who had both lost their heads.

When Wrexham Lager Beer Company was registered on 6th May 1881, it was to produce a cool sparkling lager similar to that flourishing on the Continent. The directors disliked warm English beer but failed to realise that there would be a strong prejudice against 'foreign' beer. By September 1892 the company had gone into liquidation. One of the original directors was Robert Graesser, a German-born industrial chemist who had set up a chemical works (now Monsanto plc) in Cefn and had some knowledge of lager brewing. He bought up the assets and continued to produce Wrexham Lager, the first British lager.

The drink was banned from public houses in the town. This resulted in Graesser having to sell it through privately-owned hotels and the export trade under the 'ace of clubs' trademark. At first the bottled lager thrived in the colonies and then, after 1904, the draught version was sold through American shipping lines, Cunard and White Star. It was not until the purchase of the Cross Foxes Inn during 1922, that the lager beer was available in a public house in the town.

The word 'lager' comes from the German word meaning storehouse, thus 'lagerbier' is beer for storing. Early brewing in Wrexham had been restricted to a dark lager because of difficulties with refrigeration, even though the Bavarian designers had constructed ice cellars so that cut blocks of ice could be stored for up to a year. Bavarian breweries could, at that time, depend on thicker ice for their cellars. It was not until mechanical refrigeration techniques were installed that the 'Pilsner' type of light lager was produced.

The modern logo for the company
(courtesy of Carlsberg-Tetley
Brewing Ltd)

Icehouse ruin

icehouse

OVERTON   SJ 368421

Private, no public access.

Anyone wandering around a small private woodland in Overton should beware.
There is no roof on the ruin of the Bryn-y-pys icehouse. The deep brick-lined
pit, built into the hillside is all that remains. Once it would have been filled
with ice in the winter to help preserve food, make ice-cream or chill wine.
(See CC1 p 123/4, 182) With modern refrigeration techniques it became redundant.

Bryn-y-pys Mansion (demolished 1955)

DENBIGHSHIRE AND FLINTSHIRE.

THE PARTICULARS

OF VERY EXTENSIVE, IMPORTANT AND HIGHLY VALUABLE

FREEHOLD ESTATES,

(POSSESSING GREAT POLITICAL INFLUENCE)

CONTAINING ALTOGETHER ABOUT

FOUR THOUSAND THREE HUNDRED ACRES

Of excellent Land, in a good state of Cultivation, with

SUPERIOR FARM RESIDENCES,

And all suitable Agricultural Buildings.

IN A BEAUTIFUL PART OF THE COUNTIES OF DENBIGH & FLINT,

About Three Miles from the Ruabon Station on the Shrewsbury and Chester Railway,

An easy distance from CHESTER, LIVERPOOL, MANCHESTER and other important Towns, and SIX HOURS' RIDE (per Rail) from LONDON; comprising the

CAPITAL MANSION of BRYN Y PYS

With Offices of every description, Brick-built and Stuccoed, with Portico Entrance,

AND EQUAL TO THE ACCOMMODATION OF

A NOBLEMAN OR GENTLEMAN'S FAMILY,

WITH CAPITAL WALLED GARDEN,

Woods and Plantations, forming fine Cover for Game, and the River DEE, stored with Salmon, winding its course through the Property for about Nine Miles;

Together with the Entirety or (as the case may be) the One Undivided Moiety of and in

The Manors or Lordships or reputed Manors of Overton Maddock, Bangor, & Maelor Saysnick,

IN THE COUNTY OF FLINT, for the residue of a Term of TEN THOUSAND YEARS.

But not including certain Cottages, Gardens, and small Pieces of Land, enclosed from the Wastes, within the aforesaid Manors, and which are not comprised in this Particular.

THE MANSION stands in

A FINELY UNDULATED & RICHLY WOODED PARK,

Near the centre of the Estates, upon a fine Eminence overlooking the VALLEY OF THE DEE, and commanding MAGNIFICENT VIEWS of the adjoining diversified Country, including the MOUNTAINS OF WALES.

ALSO, SEVERAL EXCELLENT RESIDENCES AND VILLAS,

WITH OFFICES AND PLEASURE GROUNDS,

AND A GREAT PORTION OF THE TOWN OF OVERTON,

One of the Flintshire Contributory Boroughs.

THIS EXTENSIVE DOMAIN is chiefly of rich Pasture and Meadow Land, divided into DAIRY FARMS, lies nearly within a ring Fence, intersected by Eight Turnpike Roads, is about *Five Miles in length* and *Three in breadth*, and contains, according to the report of an eminent Mineral Surveyor, (under the entire extent) most valuable Beds of Coal and Iron-stone.

Which will be Sold by Auction,

BY MESSRS.

FAREBROTHER, CLARK and LYE

(By direction of the TRUSTEES FOR SALE,)

At Garraway's Coffee House, 'Change Alley, Cornhill, London,

On WEDNESDAY, 13th SEPTEMBER, 1848, at 12 o'Clock,

In TWO LOTS, *(unless an acceptable Offer is previously made by Private Contract).*

Descriptive Particulars and Plans may be had Six Weeks prior to the Sale, at the Mansion; at the Office of Messrs. POTTS & BROWN, Solicitors, Chester; the Adelphi Hotel, Liverpool; Queen's Hotel, Birmingham; Albion, Manchester; at Garraway's; and at Messrs. FAREBROTHER, CLARK & LYE's Offices, No. 6, Lancaster Place, Strand, London.

J. DAVY & SONS, Printers, 137, Long Acre.

The 1848 sale particulars for the Bryn-y-pys Estate run to several pages. With most of the farms and cottages in estate hands, and no secret ballot at elections (later introduced by Gladstone), it was a point of sale that the purchaser was buying 'Great Political Influence'. This was mentioned at the top of the first page, although in the small print there is a note to say that a few cottages in the area were not owned by the estate. These private owners would have had to be strong willed to have voted against their powerful neighbours.

The remaining salt spring or brine pit at Lower Wych.

salt spring
LOWER WYCH   SJ 487442

A public path leads past the salt spring on the west bank of Iscoyd Brook.

Lower Wych is a small hamlet on the Welsh/English border. The main buildings are at Brine Pits Farm. Wych, wich or wic is Saxon for salt-town but it is likely that salt has been produced in the area around Middlewich since Roman times or before. By the Middle Ages the trade was flourishing with exports all over Britain. The Domesday Book of 1086 records the special taxes, tolls and even local laws that applied to some of the salt towns.

Farm nameplate

The earliest recorded name (11th century) for the Wych Valley is Fulewic. Other names are Foulwiche and Durtwich. There were once several pits at Lower Wych but at least one has been filled in for safety reasons. The remaining pit was said to be, "two cart ropes deep".

In the Civil War a Parliamentarian's diary recorded that, on the 28th August 1643, "Captain Croxton and Captain Venables, with their companions and others, went to Durtwich, and cut in pieces all their pans, pumps, salt-pits, and works and carried some of their pans off; so that their salt-making was spoiled, which served Shrewsbury and many other places in the kingdom." This attack, no doubt, put an end to the salt industry in Wych for a while. However, by 1831 there is a record of the 'Upper and Lower Wych Salt Works'.

victorian pump

OVERTON   SJ 374417

The pump is adjacent to the village crossroads.

Obtaining water from this village pump is difficult — a 'catch 22' situation: to pump up water you first have to prime the pump with water!

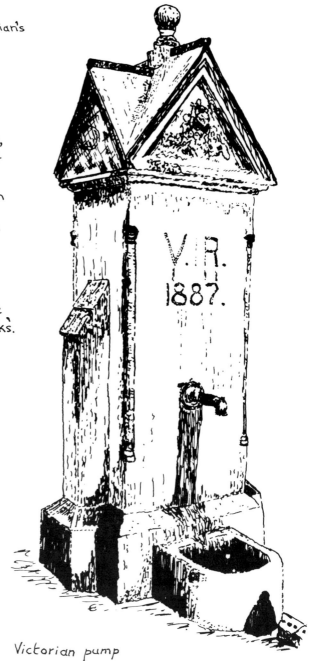

Victorian pump

hydraulic ram

LOWER WYCH   SJ489437

A public path passes the disused machinery.

The word hydraulic comes from the Greek υδρ (hydr = water) and αυλοσ (aulos = pipe). When Joseph Montgolfier (of ballooning fame) produced his first water pump he named it 'coup de belier' because it sounded like two rams' heads butting together. In English it was named a ram, perhaps also referring to the force applied to the driven water. An hydraulic ram is an automatic pump where the kinetic energy of a descending force of water in a pipe is used to raise some of that water to a height above its supply.

The 'Vulcan Ram' made by Green and Carter is one of several used along the Iscoyd and Wych brooks. Another disused ram can be found on the Maelor Way in Llan-y-cefn Wood at Overton (SJ361411).

At the end of the 19th century a 'Blake's Patent 'A' Hydraulic Ram' was installed for Philip Yorke Esq. of Erddig Park near Wrexham (SJ 324483). The engine is fed from Black Brook and pumps water to the garden 27 metres above. It is still working and can be found, along with an interpretive display, by following the park signs to the 'Cup and Saucer'. (See CC1 p139)

During the 1920's a courting couple went for a stroll through Erddig and sat down by the brook. Hearing a thump, thump, thump the girl assumed it was the boy's heart beating with passion and, having heard the warning signs, ran home in terror. (Perhaps it was his heart after all as it was their son, now retired, who related the story.)

trough

AFONWEN   SJ133714

This is beside the A541 Mold-Denbigh road.

Dated 1882, this Victorian trough was used by travellers to water their horses, cattle, donkeys, pigs and goats. Was it designed to blend in with the local hills or is it the first example of 'Art Nouveau'?

Another interesting trough stands in the market place (and car park) at Llangollen.

Victorian trough

Ffynnon Beuno

Ffynnon beuno

TREMEIRCHION   SJ084723

The public are welcome to visit this holy
well on the Tremeirchion - Bodfari road.

Henry Morton Stanley, the explorer who
met Livingstone in Africa, was born near
Denbigh Castle. According to his
autobiography (parts of which are claimed
by some to be fanciful, fantasy or even
false) he resided at Ffynnon Beuno (the
house) for a while as a child. His
description of the house and well seem
accurate:

"a few yards from the roadside
stood the inn, grocery shop, and farm-
house known as Ffynnon Beuno, - St Beuno's
Spring or Well.

"Compared with the famous
spring of St Winifred's at Holywell, that
of St Beuno is a modest affair, and boasts
of no virtues beyond purity and sweetness.

"The water is collected in a stone
tank adjoining the house of Ffynnon Beuno,
and is allowed to escape, for the benefit
of the villagers, through the open mouth
of a rude representation of a human
head, which is affixed in the front wall."

A Papyrus plant grows beside the face and
torso carved in stone at the run-off from
the well.

The procession

priests preceding papist parade picketed by placard-bearing protestants

HOLYWELL   SJ185762

The annual procession to St Winifrede's Well takes place on Midsummer's Day (June 22nd)

Pilgrims have been visiting St Winifrede's Well for over a thousand years but since Martin Luther posted his 95 theses on the Wittenburg Church door in 1517 there have been objectors to practices of the Roman Catholic Church.

The protestors

Bruce Osborne (co-author of Aque Malvernensis) testing the specific gravity of
St. Sara's Well. He also tested the temperature which, at 48°Fahrenheit, was
2° colder than other wells tested on the same day.
St Saeran on the Sepulchral stone
in Llanynys Church.

Ffynnon sara

DERWEN   SJ 064515

The well is open to the public.

There is no record of a St Sara and it is commonly
assumed that this and two other holy wells of
the same name were originally dedicated to
the sixth century St Saeran (although it is possible
that Sara was the well's custodian). The water
is said to cure cancer and rheumatism.

Source - The Holy Wells Journal is available from
Pen-y-bont, St Asaph, LL17 0HH

44

the pistyll

CAERGWRLE   SJ305575

The Pistyll gushes onto the street.

Reputedly, a never-ending supply of water issues over the carved stone in Caergwrle. Locally known as 'The Pistyll' (the waterfall), the water has fed thirsty drovers, their herds, and packhorse teams for centuries, as they approached Pont-y-delyn on their way to Chester. (See CC1 p25.)

During World War II a Mrs Dunlop evacuated to an empty house with no windows in Caergwrle. She did all the washing and cooking for her five children with water from this spring.

The Pistyll

waterfall

DYSERTH   SJ056793

A small admission charge is requested.

Dyserth Waterfall is a 20metre drop in the Afon Ffydion (also known as the Dyserth Stream) which flows from Ffynnon Asa (St Asa's Well). The water plummets over the face of a limestone escarpment at the average rate of seven tonnes a minute. The name Dyserth refers to a place of hermitage. A church, a priest, a mill and a hawk's eyrie were recorded here in 1086.

A lease for Dyserth Mill dated 20th October 1795 forbids 'the said Water Corn Grist Mill or any of the premises hereby Demised to be converted into or used as a place or places of Meeting for Methodists or any other Denomination of Sectaries'. Another document records the right to 'harvest watercrowses' from the stream, an early reference to the use of watercress as a foodstuff in North Wales.

Dyserth Waterfall

Several mills used water from the Afon Ffydion to power their waterwheels. The Pandy (woollen mill) may have had an interior undershot wheel, note the unusual roof.

waterwheel

TALLARN GREEN   SJ443443

*Access is only by permission from
Lower Tallarn Green Farm, although
a footpath passes the weir.*

Pigweed or fool's watercress grows in
the brook bellow Tallarn Green Farm.
A small weir across the brook
channelled water along a pipe to a
miniature waterwheel which pumped
water to the shippons. The wheel is
now rusted and disused but the farmer
wonders whether it would be practical
to restore it now that water metering
is being introduced.

Say,'cheese'.

The disused waterwheel

Loggerheads leat

leat and mill

LOGGERHEADS   SJ 198627

There is a parking charge at Loggerheads Country Park. Contact the information service there for opening times of the mill.

The leat or mill-race at the rear of Loggerheads Country Park Centre feeds the waterwheel of a small mill, still largely in working condition, where a small exhibition of life and work at a corn mill can be seen.

Gears in the mill

the leete

LOGGERHEADS

The famous Leete Path runs in or alongside the leat from Loggerheads to Pantymwyn.

The Leete was about 2 metres wide and 1.5 metres deep when it was cut around 1824. It was lined with puddled clay. The extensive man-made channel was built because the limestone river-bed of the River Alyn sometimes dries out. The limestone, mainly calcium carbonate, is soluble in rainwater. This results in the creation of swallow holes (sinks). The river water runs underground to reappear at lower levels, and was said to feed St Winifrede's Well at Holywell (see CC1 p115). These sinks also caused floods in local lead mines. Water from The Leete was used on a dressing floor at the Pen-y-fron Mine, for cleaning and separating the lead ore, and the run-off was used to power a waterwheel that pumped water from the mine.

The Leete and other shorter leats in the valley were mostly built for Mold Mines, a company managed by John Taylor (1779-1863) on the land of the Grosvenor family.

Mold Mines' lead output declined in the mid-19th century and the empty leat became a popular walkway.

Precipice Walk on The Leete

49

leat

DYSERTH   SJ057785

A footpath follows parts of the leat around
the hill, Carreg Heilin, behind Dyserth
Waterfall.

The Ponton Company needed water to power
their pumps and wash ores at the Meliden
Lead Mines so it bought Dyserth Mill and,
in 1754, channelled off some of the water
from the Dyserth Stream into a leat which
was cut around the hillside to the mines.

A 19th century engraving entitled 'Remains of Dyserth
Castle' shows the Dyserth leat.

Waterwheel housing at Glyndyfrdwy Slate Works

slate mines

A public footpath goes through the ruins of the old works.

Duchesses, Marchionesses, Countesses, Viscountesses, Ladies, Small Ladies, Doubles and Randoms: just some of the names given to different sizes of slates produced at the Glyndyfrdwy Slate Works. Other items produced included slabs for tombs, headstones, flagstones and chimney-pieces.

A large waterwheel housing and some sheds are all that remain of the dressing floor for both the Moel Fferna Slate Mine and the Deeside Slab Quarry. During the 19th and early 20th centuries the mine (near the Moel Fferna summit) and the quarry (a mile below the summit) produced large slabs of slate from the Ludlow and Wenlock shales present in the Berwyn Mountains. The slabs were sent down a tramway to the workshops. They were then split by hand before being planed and cut to size using machinery driven by water-power.

The men worked in teams, each known as a 'bargain' consisting of quarrymen,

The slab bridge on the footpath

Above the work area, running alongside the leat for the waterwheel are the remains of the unique 'wooden tramway.' Originally this consisted of 7ft 6ins long 6ft × 4ins rails joined by iron fish plates and separated by iron rods at regular intervals. The rails were shod with iron strips and the whole tramway was embedded in the ground. Eventually the quarry was served by a road and the tramway was left to rot. The iron strips on the rails were removed for the war effort (WWII). The quarry finally closed in 1947 and the entrances to the mine sealed by blasting.

splitters and dressers. In the quarry each bargain worked a horizontal stretch of 10 yards with a 15 yard vertical face. This was let to the bargain by the company and, in return, the finished slate was bought from the bargain by the company.

A team produced about 35 tons of finished slate in a week. In 1877 the price paid for this would have been under 7 shillings a ton. After paying rent, wages for the manager, clerks and 'trammers', as well as tools and overheads, the company would make a clear profit of about twice this amount.

leat and mill

PENLEY   SJ405398

The footpath from Penley Mill follows the old leat.

A walk along the footpath that is now part of the Maelor Way south of Penley Mill follows a wide hollow dip. This is the man-made leat to the mill. Because of the low gradient of the brook, water had to be taken off upstream and carried on an even lower gradient to provide a head of water for the corn mill. The leat became disused with the advent of other power sources. Now the mill is disused and ripe for conversion.

The leat

The mill

The twin wheels of the mill were moved apart to fit the front door in this interesting conversion.

converted mill

CEFN-Y-BEDD   SJ309560

The mill is a private residence which can be seen from the Ffrwd Road.

Cefn-y-bedd Mill was shown, still working, on television in the United States during 1962 but it was gutted by fire in 1965. This corn mill was built in 1848. Twin wheels were driven by water from the river, diverted along the leat to a launder (a large metal trough) above the wheels. When power was required, penstocks (sliding doors in the launder) were opened to allow water onto the 'overshot' water wheels.

Nant Mill with the remaining wall of what probably was a 17th century mill.

lost mills

COEDPOETH   SJ 289501

Nant Mill, signed from approach roads, is open to the public. There are picnic tables, and a variety of events throughout the year. Contact Wrexham Tourist Office for details.

The still-existing two-storey corn mill was built during 1831 and 1832 by John Price, the miller, with a grant of £1,000 from the owner of Plas Power Estate, Thomas Fitzhugh. When the new mill was completed in 1832, it had two wooden overshot water-wheels, although from the turn of the century until 1940 a steel 'Pelton wheel' turbine, less than two metres in diameter, was driven by piped water. A previous mill alongside had been worked by John Price since at least 1818.

However, the tithe map of 1851 shows, as well as the mill pond, three buildings on the site: one beside the present mill and one in front of it. It is likely that all three were mills from different centuries but unfortunately, in a catalogue of errors, both the other mills were destroyed.

1645 A letter from Sir Robert Middleton mentions a 'Nant-y-Pandu' (valley of the fulling or woollen mill).

1770 A map shows one mill on the Nant Mill site, position unclear.

1818 John Price worked a corn mill at the Nant.

1831 Nant Bridge was built.

1832 Price completed the new mill (now called Nant Mill and open to the public).

1851 Tithe map shows a mill pond, three buildings on site, and two 'Pandy Fields'.

1905 A renowned local historian, A N Palmer, wrote 'The Nant Mill was further up the stream [from Bersham] and was a fulling mill, so that the Nant itself was called Nant-y-Pandu'. Palmer went on to say that a pandy was in 'the Pandy Fields [below Nant Bridge] stretching down to the river. I find the "pandy" walk mill, or fulling house that stood here mentioned in the rate books in the year 1752 and again in 1813'. Note that Palmer referred to a pandy in the past tense.

Palmer then stated that Nant Mill was a pandy. Either this was an error or there had been two pandies close to each other. Why didn't Palmer mention the still-working Corn Mill?

1970s Nant Mill was purchased by Wrexham Rural District Council. The building in front of the mill had been used as a shippon for cattle but had blocked up doors and windows. The tenant took the roof, which he had put on, with him when he was evicted. Vandals damaged the building and the council removed the roof beams and parts of the walls for safety despite the prior tenant's claim that, 'there's more history in this old building than in your Nant Mill'.

1970s A stone stile inscribed 'to the healing well' was lost when council workmen rebuilt the wall at the southern entrance to the mill.

1980s   Bersham Heritage Centre published a history of the mill claiming (wrongly) that Nant Mill was built on the site of the previous mill. The leaflet also repeated Palmer's statement that Nant Mill had been a pandy suggesting that this had been in the place of the present building.

1990/91   Wrexham Maelor BC refurbished the 1832 mill as a visitor centre, still suggesting it had been a pandy, and even putting a description of a pandy's workings on a signboard inside. (The records for the 1832 mill and its design are clearly for a corn mill.) The walls in front of the building were lowered and stabilised. The remaining walls of a sandstone building beside the mill were removed and a brick shed constructed in its place.

1993   Bersham Heritage Centre published 'The Clywedog Trail' and repeated that, "The mill stands on the former site of a fulling mill or pandy"

1994   More of the old building's walls were removed.

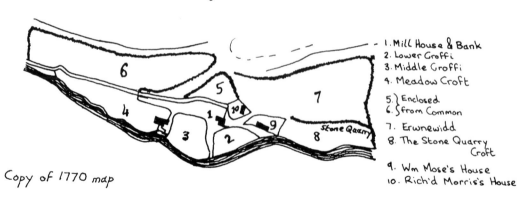

1. Mill House & Bank
2. Lower Groffi
3. Middle Groffi
4. Meadow Croft

5.) Enclosed
6.) from Common
7. Erwnewidd
8. The Stone Quarry Croft

9. Wm Mose's House
10. Rich'd Morris's House

Copy of 1770 map

Clearly the 'pandy' was recorded downstream in the pandy fields below Nant Mill. The building beside Nant Mill (where the brick shed is) was the previous corn mill. We may never know if the building in front of the present mill (one wall remains) was the original corn mill, the miller's house, or another pandy. A weir on the river suggests that there was a leat to an undershot wheel. Almost certainly it was the oldest building on the site and yet no archaeological work was done on site before demolition even though it was a council-owned property empty for years — curious or careless.

Circular buddle with heather and flannel sweep arms

lead mines

MINERA   SJ 274509

Minera Lead Mines and the restored engine house are open to the public. Children (and adults) can try separating the silver crystals of Galena from a dust mixture.

Visitors to Minera Lead Mines can now see the process used for washing and separating lead ore with a working reconstruction. Much of the dressing floor beside the Meadow Shaft had been covered with spoil heaps. When the spoil was removed ore storage bins were discovered, probably the only intact ones in Britain.

The product and waste from each stage of dressing were quite different from the preceding stage. The waste tips contain clues as to which dressing processes were undertaken at a mine. Productivity and age can also be ascertained.

The primary tips found close to the head of the shaft contain large uncrushed pieces of rock, generally barren of valuable minerals, from the initial shaft sinking and tunnel driving. Drill holes from blasting preparations are commonly found in the waste rock.

The first stage of the lead extraction process at Minera was to remove the large lumps of ore, which was almost pure galena, from lumps of rock. This was done on the 'picking grates'. The ore was then broken smaller with an iron 'bucking' hammer, and again picked over. Water washed the dusty particles of ore into 'trunk buddles'. The coarse lumps of mixed ore were crushed between two 14 inch rollers, producing gravel size pieces to be treated in the 'jig boxes'. Sandy sized material from the jigs and trunk buddle were conveyed to the centre of the circular convex buddle. The sweep arms were fitted with heather as an agitator and flannel as a smoother. The heavy lead ore stayed at the centre of the buddle while the lighter limestone was washed to the outside.

The jig boxes produced a washed gravel which proved ideal for making concrete and for general building purposes. The white calcite waste was used locally for pebble dashing. The buddles produced a slimy waste which reacted with the lime materials to set like concrete on the tips. After the mine closed, the Minera Mines and Gravel Company worked from 1915 to 1950 to exploit what had been the mine's waste product.

There are only two restored Cornish Beam Engine Houses in the world. The other is at the Burra Burra Mine in Australia.

Galena occurs as cubic crystals which readily crumble into small cubes when struck. It contains up to 87% lead and 0.5% silver.

windmill

HOLYWELL   SJ 151758

The mill is a private residence.

Pen-y-maes (top-of-the-field) Windmill was erected
in the mid-18th century for the Cotton Trust Company.
With a ten metre diameter base and walls almost
a metre thick it stands to a height of about 17
metres. Payment to the miller was made at a
rate of 10% of the grain milled. The windmill
closed in 1890 and was left empty for many
years before being converted into a residence.

Other windmills once stood on Halkyn Mountain,
in Bettisfield (see CC1 p 34) and in Denbigh

Holywell Windmill

Denbigh, an 1830 engraving drawn by Gastineau, engraved by Radclyffe, showing the windmill.

mill and stables

EYTON

SJ 350453

Craft shops, restaurant and a caravan site can be found at The Plassey. The Stables Coffee Shop is open to the public all year for morning coffee, light lunches and afternoon teas.

The Plassey at Eyton lies on a moated site (the moat was still visible in 1911) dating from at least the 16th century and possibly medieval times. The Domesday Book records that 'St Chads held Eitune before [1066] although before that 'King Edward [the Confessor] gave to King Gruffydd [of Wales] all the land' this side of the River Dee. 'But when King Gruffydd wronged him, he took this land from him and gave it back to the Bishop of Chester and to all his men, who had formerly held it'. There was '1 hide (about 40 acres of arable land), 1 fishery, meadow ½ acre, woodland 2 acres'. The value was 5s.

At a later date a hall was probably built next to a pre-existing building resulting in the name 'Y Plasau' (the halls). Over the years the name became anglicised.

In 1902 Frank Lloyd bought the estate to complement his business. In 1890 he had acquired an auctioneer's business and built stables for 300 horses together with a show ring and trotting track behind the Wynnstay Arms in Wrexham. Over 1500 horses could be sold in a day at his monthly auctions. At The Plassey he expanded the existing house and built the model dairy. Above the stables was a feed storage loft. A mill was found on refurbishment.

The present owners have owned the estate since 1960. Over the years they proceeded to convert the farm buildings into craft shops, a coffee shop and a restaurant, retaining and enhancing the original features, and hanging pictures of Frank Lloyd in the Visitor Centre. Not only did the conversion win awards from the Royal Institute of Chartered Surveyors and the Country Landowners' Association, but a new beer, Plassey Ale, brewed in the rear of the building won two commendations from Camra. If you are curious why, the ale can be tasted at the restaurant.

Stables Coffee Shop

cocoa & reading rooms

OVERTON   SJ 373416

The rooms are now the public library.

In an effort to prevent alcoholism and help educate the populace in the village of Overton, the Bryn-y-pys Estate, in conjunction with the local temperance association, erected this terracotta building in 1890. Hot cocoa was brewed next door and brought in for customers. Cocoa-taverns and cocoa-rooms became popular countrywide at the end of the 19th century. (A similar club and cocoa house was built at Bagillt in 1883.) They were promoted by temperance societies and by Quakers who controlled much of the cocoa market, including Cadburys. Their influence resulted in Quaker-owned newspapers being referred to as the 'cocoa-press'.

A new movement for Gospel Temperance in Britain was promoted by an American, Richard Booth, during 1882. Richard Cadbury, guaranteeing all costs, invited him to speak in Birmingham. John Cadbury, Richard's ailing father who had been leader of a similar movement in Birmingham, also spoke on several occasions. In three weeks of meetings over 50,000 pledges of total abstinence were made and a Gospel Temperance Mission set up. Richard Cadbury was a lifelong supporter. On 22nd October 1889 he opened a Temperance Institute which became the home of the UK Alliance, the Band of Hope, the Sunday Closing Association, the Church of England Temperance Society, the National Vigilance Association and others. The Institute housed a large number of books. Total abstainers subscribing for five shillings annually had access to the Institute and its library.

The name cocoa derives from the three syllable word 'cacao' used until the 18th century. This came from the Spanish and like the word chocolate was derived from the Mayan 'xocoatl' (choco=foam or bitter, atl = water or bean according to different authorities). The Aztecs, who founded Mexico in 1325, imported 'cacahuitl' for drinking. Hernando Cortez met (and later killed) the Aztec Emperor of Mexico in the early 16th century and found that chocolate, flavoured with honey and vanilla was Emperor Montezuma's only beverage and that he drank it before visiting his wives, leading to the assumption that it was an aphrodisiac. The Spanish cultivated cacao trees and kept the chocolate recipe a secret until the beginning of the 17th century. A 'chocolate house' was opened during London during 1657. By the end of the century chocolate was being sold in London for around £1 a kilo so that 'none but the rich and famous could afford to drink choclatl'.

At the end of the 18th century Dr Joseph Fry of Bristol used a steam engine to grind cocoa beans. A Dutch pressing machine was designed by Van Heuten to create cocoa butter in 1828 – used by Cadburys in 1866 to produce pure cocoa powder. Frys made the first commercial chocolate bar in 1847. Milk chocolate was brought into production by Nestle in 1876, and fondant, which melted on the tongue, by Lindt in 1879.

At Chirk, Cadbury's factory processes over 50,000 tonnes of cocoa beans annually. After sorting and cleaning, the beans are roasted before kibbling (breaking) and winnowing (removing the husks) to produce cocoa 'nibs'. These are combined into a 'mass' containing over half its weight in cocoa butter. When half this butter is removed, and the remaining cake crushed, it results in cocoa powder. Eating chocolate is created from the mass by further processing.

The unusual library at Overton.

The Pigeonaire, Penley

buildings

PENLEY, ESCLUSHAM, ABERGELE   SJ416405, SJ283481, SH946763

There is no public access to the Penley buildings, the others can be seen from public paths.

Which of these buildings is the odd one out? 'A rebuilt Former Georgian Pigeon House in semi-rural location on the fringe of the village affording two bedroomed

Converted Stables, Penley

Tan-y-lan, Esclusham

accommodation set in large arboured garden'. The Pigeonaire was sold by Wingetts in 1995. It had been part of Penley Hall and attached to the stables (also converted) but was moved and converted into an unusual detatched residence. The Pumphouse is an interesting conversion from a public utility building, whilst Tan-y-lan, the cruck house in Esclusham is believed to date from 1565 and is still a private house.

Converted Pumphouse, Abergele

Madras School

madras school

PENLEY   SJ412400

The building can be seen from the main road.

The Reverend Andrew Bell, an army chaplain at Madras, evolved a system of teaching whereby older students were employed as teachers or 'monitors' of younger children. It was first used in Britain in 1789. In 1811 the 'National Society for the Education of the Poor in the principles of the Established Church' was formed using Bell's 'Madras' system. Their schools were in competition with those of the 'British and Foreign Schools Society' which used the system of Joseph Lancaster, promoted mainly by Quakers.

By 1851 there were 17,015 National schools as opposed to 1,500 British schools. As vice-president of the National Society, Lord Kenyon (II) lost no time in founding a Madras school in Penley during 1811. He gave the land and paid for the building and its teachers. Other Madras schools were built at nearby Overton, Tallarn Green (later moved to Threapwood) and Ellesmere.

A Bronze Age school perhaps? This thatched hut can be found at Legacy Environmental Education Centre run by Groundwork Wrexham.

68

schools

GWAENYSGOR   SJ076811

Both village schools are now closed; one is a private residence, the other is a community centre.

The Gwaenysgor school opened on Tuesday 24th January 1905 with 33 children. Sewing and drawing was taught on a Tuesday, knitting and drawing on Thursday. The school closed on 31st May 1909.

An artifact kept at the Hawarden Record Office and produced on request is a trowel in perfect condition. The silver-plated trowel was used to lay the mortar for the foundation stone of the new council school which took over from the old school after it opened in 1907 causing some friction between the staff and villagers.

Yr Hen Ysgol (the old school)

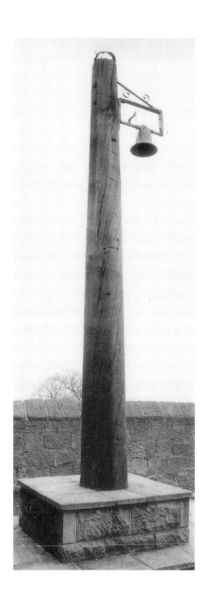

bell and mast

PENTRE BROUGHTON   SJ 302534

The school yard is usually open outside school hours.

A bell on a ship's mast was used in Black Lane Colliery to ring time for shifts. Black Lane School is named after the colliery and has the bell and mast in the school yard.

Black Lane Bell and Mast

The services bell

old vicarage
RUABON   SJ304435

Now split into three private homes, the old vicarage can be seen from the nearby road.

It is said that there were once two bells on the roof of the old vicarage. One to announce when services were held there and one to call the labourers in from the fields. It was once the 'Mansion House'. In 1636 it had an orchard and garden with a brewhouse and two barns. In the 18th century the Reverend Davies cast 60,000 bricks to make repairs. By 1856 the vicarage had 11 bedrooms inside the main building. Outside were stables, a cowhouse and calf-kit, a cart-house, coach house, saddle room and stables.

The property was also the home of Major Walton Clapham Wingfield who first published the rules of 'Σθαιριστικη' (spherestick) or Lawn Tennis in 1874.

parliament house
RHUDDLAN   SJ023781

This is a private house in the main street.

In 1277 Edward I marched from Chester and seized Rhuddlan from the Welsh Prince Llewelyn. He built the stone castle and arranged the town beside it. Another Welsh uprising in 1282, by Dafydd (Llewelyn's half-brother who had changed sides) and Llewelyn damaged the castle but repairs were made during the next few years.

The inscription on Parliament House states that the Statute of Wales was issued from here in 1284. The statute, now held in the Record Office, created the shires of the new counties which lasted, largely unchanged, until 1974. Rhuddlan was originally in Flintshire, it later became part of Clwyd and is now in the new county of Denbighshire. The truth of the local legend that a parliament was held in this building is doubted by some historians. Hubbard in 'The Buildings of Wales: Clwyd' claims that the 13th century doorway and 14th century cusped ogee (pointed double-curved stonework) are ex situ and from the castle.

Parliament House

72

'Valle Crucis Abbey'

landmarks

LLANGOLLEN   SJ420422

Children will enjoy this short tour, open weekends and school holidays from Easter to September.

After climbing through the ruins of the famous Castell Dinas Brân, you visit the gorsedd (stone circle) and the 'Ladies' house at Plas Newydd. Continue through Valle Crucis Abbey, go under the Chain Bridge but avoid the treacherous Horseshoe Falls. Watch out for steam trains in the Rhysgôg Tunnel on your return from Berwyn. Go over Bishop Trevor Bridge at Llangollen, then through the white water under it. Travel the World's End road on Ruabon Mountain and tunnel through the slate mines before cruising along the longest crazy golf hole in the world, the Llangollen Canal, complete with Telford's Aqueduct.

Roger Goodman hired part of the Riverside Park and built his Landmark Novelty Golf in 1992. The obstacles on the course are models of historical features in and around the Vale of Llangollen.

73

The entrance to the wedding cave

wedding cave
BWLCHGWYN

Some of the steps to the cave are deteriorating.

A series of limestone caves can be found in the beautiful Ffrith Valley. Some are natural or partly natural, others have been mined for lead over the ages. In 1850 a Liverpool tea merchant, Thomas Fry, built a hunting lodge in the valley. He sold it to Mr Peek, another tea merchant. The improved building was then sold to R.V. Kyrke, a local ironmaster. Now called Nant-y-Ffrith Hall, it passed through two generations to the heiress Mrs Spottiswoode, whose upbringing in the Welsh foothills was the base for her explorations. In 1908 she became the first white woman to cross the Andes. Over the years Nant-y-Ffrith, its caves, and its reservoir shown on picture postcards, were visited by thousands of people. This led the owner, in 1909, to erect notices: 'Persons from Wrexham and elsewhere visiting Nant-y-Ffrith are requested by the owner to behave like his neighbours at Bwlchgwyn, namely, as ladies and gentlemen and not to shout and scream on the drive or throw orange peel and papers about. Anyone breaking the trees and shrubs or stealing ferns or plants will be prosecuted.'

When a group of girls from St Mary's Church in Chester visited in the 1920s, they were given tea, and lent candles to explore the caves. The unusual name for the largest cave comes from a wedding reception held inside it.

pontnewydd cave

ST ASAPH   SJ015710

There is no public access to the site.

A quarter of a million years ago, before the last Ice Age, Neolithic hunter-gatherers probably followed wild herds of animals across the land bridge from the Continent to what is now Britain. With no customs and no immigration laws, and a lack of rentable accommodation, some of these people found suitable habitation in the Elwy Valley. Sitting in or outside their natural shelter they produced, over the years, a fascinating collection of stone tools such as handaxes, spearpoints and scrapers for skins, little knowing that when they died their bones would go down in history as those of the first people recorded in Wales.

The archaeological remains and signs of hibernating bears were carried to the rear of the cave in mud flows.

Further reading: Archaeology of Clwyd pub. Clwyd CC
Neandertal, National Geographic Jan. '96

In World War II the cave was used as an ammunition store, thus its walled entrance.

bomb shelter

OVERTON   SJ 376408

The top of the shelter can be seen from a nearby footpath, the interior by request to Lightwood Hall. There may be a charge.

Down the hatch

All hands below

This might have become the home of the last people in Wales. It was built by the Air Ministry after the Second World War as a control and communications centre in case of nuclear attack. The shelter replaced a lookout tower in a nearby field. First known as post 26.02 it later became R.O.C. post 16.N.4 Overton. The 0.042 acres of land were leased at £1 per annum. Occupants would not have lasted long if the bomb had been dropped nearby. Although seven metres underground and protected from an initial blast, the shelter had only relatively short-term food supplies for its occupants, no lead shielding and several airducts. Log books record inspections of the shelter, although most other equipment has been removed. The local farmer, from whom the land was leased, has now been given the empty bunker and intends to keep it as an historical curiosity.

Lime kiln

The kiln is adjacent to a path from Abergele to Tower Hill.

Limestone taken from the escarpment above the kiln was crushed and burnt here at a temperature of over 900° Celsius. The process releases carbon dioxide (44% by weight of the original mass) leaving calcium oxide, otherwise known as lime or quick-lime. The powder, when mixed with water is known as slaked or hydrated lime. It was used as a whitewash for walls and ceilings, as well as a building mortar. Lime is also used as an acidity regulator in agriculture.

When transportation methods improved, lime was produced at larger quarries leaving lime kilns of various types to fall into ruin. This kiln became known as 'the cave' and was used as a home by a hermit called 'Ferguson' before 1940.

The limekiln known as 'the cave'

Looking out from the cave.

st beuno's cave

TREMEIRCHION   SJ086724

Access is by permission only, from Fynnon Beuno.

Professor Boyd Dawkins excavated St Beuno's Cave at the end of the 19th century.
Found within were the bones of lion, wild cat, spotted hyaena, wolf, fox, bear,
badger, wild boar, bovid, Irish deer, red deer, roebuck, reindeer, horse, woolly
rhinoceros and mammoth. A predomination of hyaena bones suggest that these
predators used it as a den and it is unlikely that a mammoth walked in.
Traces of human habitation from around 30,000 – 40,000 BC were also found
including scrapers and other flint tools. Mining trials took place in the
cave during more modern times. Outside the cave is one of the few sites
in North Wales where milk thistle can be found.

wood anemone

CILCAIN   SJ 184641

Wood anemone can be seen in many North Wales' woodlands.

A delicate windflower or wood anemone grew in the roadside verge near Cilcain. Although these beautiful plants are not curious to Clwyd, it is rare to find them on the roadside. More often they are found in woods as their name suggests, and they are an indicator of ancient woodland rather than softwood plantations from the 20th century or even beechwoods from the 18th century.

Interestingly the species has evolved with large sepals rather than petals. The plant can, according to textbooks, have between five and eight sepals. However plants in the Clywedog Valley, Wrexham, tend to have five sepals, whereas six sepals can be seen in plants on Mold Mountain. The wood anemone from Cilcain, a roadside reminder of how country hedges can protect a valuable wealth of flora, has eight. Goronwy Wynne's 'Flora of Flintshire' comments on an unusual variant, "a plant with purple flowers was recorded near Loggerheads in 1975."

Eight-sepalled Wood Anemone head

black poplar

The tree is beside the lane north of the church.

It is now rare to find black poplars although they were once a distinctive feature of lowland river valleys. The black poplar was once a favourite timber tree but was superseded by faster growing hybrids after the mid-18th century. *Populus nigra betufolia* grows to 30 metres but the tree does not seem to be regenerating naturally and is now the most endangered native timber tree in Britain. (For example only about 200 survive in nearby Cheshire.) Its dark brown bark is full of bosses making interesting and curious shapes. The name may come from this bark colouration, darker foliage than the white poplar, or even from the black circle seen at the centre of its trunk when felled.

Langham, in 1579, recommended that 'the leaves and young buds of black Poplar, stampt and applyed, swageth the paine of the gout in the hands or feet.' Culpeper, in his 17th century herbal, states that a sweet type of musk growing on the tree was once used in ointments. The grim dark nature of the tree was said to be of a Saturnine nature: all herbs were given a planet to govern them. Culpeper directs, "To such as study astrology (who are the only men I know that are fit to study physic, physic without astrology, being like a lamp without oil)... Fortify the body with herbs of the nature of the ascendant. ... Let your medicine be something anti-pathetical to the Lord of the Sixth."

Before today's newspaper 'sun sign astrology' became popular, a practitioner would find a person's ascending astrological sign by their place, time and date of birth. They could then find the sixth house which is said to relate to matters of personal health. It was claimed that an incorrect balance, causing illness, could be remedied by prescribing the correct astrological herb. Thus someone with Cancer or Libra in the Ascendant had Sagittarius or Pisces respectively in the sixth house. As both of these were ruled by Jupiter the person would be given a herb of Saturn (anti-pathetic or opposite in astrological nature) to cure them.

rock formation

RHEWL   SJ107548

The rocks can be seen from a public foot path.

Water from the Clywedog has eroded the mudstone shales on its banks into mysterious rock formations.

The public path on the other bank is known as Lady Bagot's Drive after the 17th century lady who regularly drove along it to Bontuchel in her coach.

In the latter part of the 19th century the London and North Western Railway Company planned to extend their line from Rhewl to Cerrig-y-drudion along the riverbank. The line was never completed even though, as the Denbighshire Historical Society Transactions record, one man went on working even after the plans were axed.

Mysterious rock formations on the Clywedog

The stone circle is a gorsedd built to commemorate the 1923 National Eisteddfod

bailey hill

MOLD   SJ 234643

A path leads to the summit

Mold, the English name for Clwyd's former county town, derives from Mont Alto (high hill); its Welsh name, Yr Wyddgrug, roughly translates as burial mound, presumably referring to Bailey Hill. The hill is the site of a Norman castle. No excavations have been made in the motte at the summit so it is unknown whether or not the high mound that supported the motte was built on a pre-existing burial site. Almost certainly the mound is man-made. The motte-and-bailey (wooden castle and stockade) was the stronghold of Robert de Montalt, under the Earl of Chester. In 1147 it was captured by Owain Glyndŵr but returned to the Montalt family for several generations despite being taken twice more by Welsh Princes. Llewelyn (the last) held it from 1256–1276.

trevor rocks
LLANGOLLEN   SJ 233432

View from the southern side of the Vale of Llangollen.

Trevor Rocks are not in Trevor but in Llangollen. They are part of the Eglwyseg Escarpment on the north side of the Dee Valley. The escarpment consists of limestone formed 290-350 million years ago in the Carboniferous Age, as a coral reef in tropical water. This reef then underwent an enormous uplift caused by the warming of the shales previously formed in the Silurian Age, 405-440 million years ago. It was men from Trevor who gave the name to the rocks as they quarried the limestone, using tramways to transport the mineral to the road and, more importantly, the canal. The inclined plane trackway beds can still be seen.

Trevor Rocks on the Eglwyseg Escarpment and Dinas Brân

The majority of the surface rock on Ruabon Mountain is Cefn-y-fedw sandstone which formed in layers on top of the limestone. Nearby, under the famous castle ruins, Dinas Brân has a different geological structure. This small hill consists of an outlier of Upper Salopian shales from the Silurian Age, the same shales that form part of the Berwyn Mountains on the south side of the valley. The present shape of the hill is the result of a glacier from the last Ice Age, 10,000 – 15,000 years ago, which gouged out the U-shaped valley that the River Dee now runs through.

Another effect of the glacier was to carve the Dee Valley in a northerly direction whereas formerly the water had gone south, through the area where Chirk now stands and into the Severn.

millstone

CAERGWRLE

A path from the war memorial leads to Caergwrle Castle.

The first stone castle in Caergwrle was built by Dafydd ap Gruffydd. Edward I gave him the cantref of Hope and 100 marks, 'for the building of his castle at Kaierguill'. Later, Dafydd joined his half-brother Llewelyn in attacking the English. Three months afterwards the King's army arrived to find the castle dismantled by the retreating Welsh.

Edward rebuilt the castle using about 30 masons and 340 carpenters. He gave it to his consort, Eleanor, but two years later it burnt down. Despite several grants to various lords by the Crown, the castle was never repaired. Stone was taken to other buildings and a band of itinerant masons realised that the bedrock under the castle consisted of millstone-grit; this was ideal, needless to say, for making millstones — which they did. The millstones were carved directly out of the ground. At least one had a fault in it, and it can still be found about ten metres below the southern corner of the castle.

Millstone

millstone

HOPE   SJ309583

The church is in the centre of the
village.

Compare the millstone built
into the side of Hope Church
with that below Caergwrle
Castle. When the church was
rebuilt the masons used any
handy stone, including a zig-zag
stone below the bell tower, and
tombstones inscribed with
Celtic crosses in the south
and north walls.

A zig-zag stone in the bell tower
is said to be of Norman or Saxon
origin.

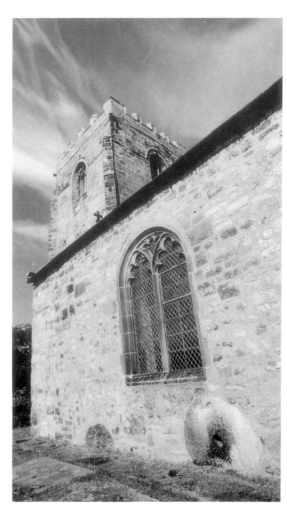

Millstone in the church wall.

cup stone

CORWEN   SJ079433

The churchyard is open during the day.

The preaching cross outside Corwen
Church is now just a pillar, the cross
that formed the top missing, similar
to Eliseg's Pillar in Valle Crucis (see
CC1 page 40) but the Corwen cross is
believed to date from the 12th century.

At the base of the shaft is a round
stone with possible cupmarks. Cup
and ring marks appear on cromlechau
and standing stones all over Europe.
The Reverend Elias Owen in his book,
'Old Stone Crosses of the Vale of Clwyd',
now republished by Clwyd County
Council, points out that 204 marked
stones had been found in Scotland
and 100 in England but only 2 in
Wales.

*Further reading: A Land of Gods and
Giants by Mick Sharp pub. Fraser Stewart
Book Wholesale Ltd.*

*The interlaced design at the top of
the cross shaft has been claimed to
be based on a Viking design like that
on Maen Achwyfan cross (see CC1 p 82).*

Kneeling Stone

kneeling stones
CORWEN

SJ079433

The church is behind the main street.

One theory about these strangely cut stones at the foot of graves in Corwen churchyard is that they were kneeling stones. It was customary for mourners to kneel at the foot of the grave to pray for the soul of the dear departed. What more useful than a kneeling stone made to measure by the local mason? For the child of the departed the hollows had to be closer, leading to three curves being cut on some stones. The kneeling stone may have been the profitable idea of a Corwen mason, for this unusual feature is unique to this area. Similar stones can be seen at nearby Llangar Church.

Kneeling Stones

Llangar Church

death
LLANGAR   SJ 063424

It is well worth visiting the church but you need to arrange entry and pay admission fees at Rug Chapel near Corwen.

The original name of this small church near Corwen is said to be Llan-garw-gwyn (the church of the white stag). In legend a prophecy foretold that the church should be built where a white stag started (where a male deer jumped and ran). Outside the church are several raised tombs, probably built because of the rocky surface of the graveyard.

Inside are box pews, a rare pyramidal music stand and wall paintings from several centuries. The huge figure of Death is prominent: a skeleton with an arrow and a winged hour-glass. It probably dates from the early 19ᵗʰ century.

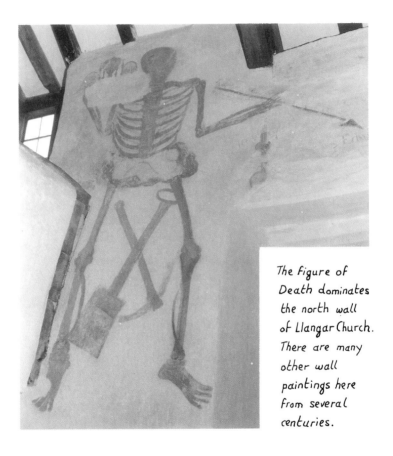

The figure of
Death dominates
the north wall
of Llangar Church.
There are many
other wall
paintings here
from several
centuries.

Wall painting of Death at Rug Chapel

death

CORWEN   SJ 064439

Rug Chapel, signposted from the A5 northwest of Corwen, has an admission charge.

The highly decorated chapel at Rug was built in 1637 for Colonel William Salusbury. As a Royalist in the Civil War he held Denbigh Castle for 3 years, whilst under seige from the Parliamentarians.

The interior of the chapel contains items of varied interest, including carvings of animals and mythical creatures on the single planks of oak used as bench ends in the aisle. There is also a seventeenth century wall painting depicting death: a fine looking well-to-do skeleton which even has a pillow of rope. As well as an hour glass there is a dial with 'time flies' in Latin. Another Latin inscription suggests that 'life passes by the hour'.

The verse of a Welsh carol proclaims that 'as the candle burns, life on Earth turns' with yet another reminder below stating 'how ever long your life is, it will end one day'. The third line in Welsh is from a poem and describes the sorry state of a skeleton whose face has rotted, has lost its wits and is unknown. Finally a Welsh proverb states 'every strong one is weak in the end'.

A comprehensive guide to both Rug and Llangar is available at Rug Chapel or by post from CADW: Welsh Historic Monuments, Brunel House, 2 Fitzalen Road, CARDIFF CF2 1UY

The bench end carvings in Rug Chapel date from the 17th century. This part of the north aisle bench includes (from left to right): a sheep, a cow's face with serpents, two dragons.

Founder's Tomb

founder's tomb

HANMER   SJ 454396

The tomb can be found beside the north wall of the church.

After the architect had completed the church at Hanmer
it is said that he fell to his death from the tower.

The church building has also suffered from catastrophe.
In 1463, a century after Owain Glyndŵr was married
here, the church burnt down and was not rebuilt

The churchyard cross was carved with scenes of the crucifixion, a bishop, the Virgin and Child, and the Virgin and St John.

The cross was knocked down by the Parliamentarians in the Civil War and was not re-erected until 1739 when '10s2d' was paid 'for setting ye cross stright'.

Old engraving

until 1490 (by the founder). Later, in the Civil War, the preaching cross was knocked down by the Parliamentarians and was not re-erected until 1739. In 1889 the church burnt down again. Luckily the Reverend Lee (a keen historian who had written two volumes of notes on Hanmer's history) saved some of the church registers from the blaze.

cross

YSCEIFIOG   SJ15214

The preaching cross stands at the rear of the central village church.

The churchyard cross in the small village of Ysceifiog stands in a poor condition, shaft upright and head on the floor. Its base is said to bear the incisions of arrow heads. In Plantaganet times the villagers, by royal command, practised archery in the churchyard during Sundays and holidays, and sharpened their arrows on any handy stone.

After 1345 landowners earning £5 per annum had to supply an archer to the king for the war in France. British archery skills paid off on 26th August 1346 at the Battle of Crecy where four thousand of the French army were slaughtered. The crossbow of the French was a complex instrument, wieldy, slow and heavy to carry but was used despite being banned by the church in 1139.

Cross (above) with arrow marks (below)

cross

DENBIGH   SJ052660

Look beside the library to find this.

The Denbigh high cross bears the
marks of a variety of uses. As
well as being used as a lamppost,
the cross had holes to affix
market shuttering which was
supported on it by day and tied to
it at night. The market butchers
made another use of it. Carving
the meat took its toll on the
tools of the trade, and the sandstone
body of the cross shaft was an
ideal sharpener. The cross is now
beside the disused town stocks.

Denbigh High Cross.

war memorial

PENYCAE   SJ 242485

Walk across Ruabon Mountain on the public path from World's End or the mountain gate Penycae to reach the stone cross. There are no public paths by Mountain Lodge.

The horizontal stone cross at the summit of Ruabon Mountain marks where a Bristol Beaufighter hit the mountain during the Second World War. Records show the grim death toll of young inexperienced pilots and crew on this mountain.

Some of the other crashes that occured were:

5th February 1941, Fairy Fulmar – pilot killed
3rd July 1941, 2 Spitfires – both pilots killed
16th November 1941, Spitfire – pilot killed
29th January 1942, Hurricane – pilot killed
21st August 1942, Anson – pilot and 3 crew killed
30th January 1944, Oxford – pilot killed
31st August 1944, Spitfire – pilot killed

There are another 5 recorded crashes.

The mountain was used as a decoy for bombers. On 29th August 1940 bombs meant for Liverpool were dropped on the mountain and 72 square kilometres burnt in a fire so huge that clouds of dust and soot reached Manchester. Some bombs fell on Rhosllanerchrugog causing casualties and one destroyed Plas Ucha in Penycae. Plas Ucha at World's End suffered damage.

In 1943 the army detonated explosives, damaging local buildings. The following year a man was seriously injured after treading on a grenade left from training. After the war the mountain was believed to have been cleared of unexploded bombs – twice! The second time was after a walker found another bomb. Yet people continue to find aeroplane wreckage and bombs in the area. In 1988 part of a Martinet piloted by a Polish airman was recovered. An unexploded bomb was found in May 1989. Metal detecting on the mountain is not recommended.

Bristol Beaufighter
Used for night interception
of raiders with its Airborne
Interception Radar.

Frozen clock

PENYCAE   SJ 255452

A public footpath passes the ruin.

Just south of Newtown Mountain, on the bulk that is known generally as Ruabon Mountain, is Frozen Clock. This was once used as a base for the broom making industry in Penycae. A company was formed by George Jackson and his two brothers. The material for the brooms or besoms, in this case heather and not broom, was collected on the moor, and grug (heather) dues were paid to Sir Watkin Williams Wynn for this privilege. The brooms manufactured here were dispatched by rail to Liverpool and Glasgow from Rhosllanerchrugog Station. They were the exported as far as the Continent and the USA.

The building's curious name may have originated when Sir Watkin, who often called in while grouse shooting, commented that this location was so high up that, "your clock must be frozen". A local man relating a similar story stated that his grandmother, when asked the time by Sir Watkin, gave the reply, "Cloc wedi rhewi" (the clock is frozen). Yet another story is that when the building was used by quarry workers the clock froze and the workers continued into another shift. When they realised what had happened they asked for more pay and, being refused, they went on strike.

Frozen Clock Ruin by Andy Ross

column
RUABON

Access to the woodland is by permission from the Cefn Estate Office, Plas yn Cefn, St Asaph.

FILIO OPTIMO MATER – SVPERSTES

'For the best son from his still-living mother' reads the Latin inscription on the impressive 36 metre high fluted column almost hidden in the woodland of Wynnstay Park. The memorial was for the fourth baronet, Sir Watkin Williams-Wynn. His ancestor, Sir John Wynn had renamed the area from Watstay (after Wat's Dyke, the eighth century ditch and dyke passing through the estate).

The nearby house was built mainly for the third baronet in the 18th century but alterations were still in hand in the mid-19th under the sixth baronet. A fire destroyed the mansion in 1858. Much of the family fortune in paintings, rare manuscripts and jewellery was destroyed. 'Meetings of Condolence' were frequently held in the area afterwards and, at a public meeting in Wrexham, it was suggested by the vicar that people from all over the country should subscribe towards buying Lady Williams-

The Column

Wynn a new casket of jewels! The house was rebuilt by 1866. In 1950 a private school, Lindisfarne College, took over the property. This recently closed and the house was sold during 1995. Furniture and school possessions were auctioned.

memorial

The stone is part of the road kerb above Bronwylfa on the east side.

Kerb Memorial

The inscription 7-1913 on this unobtrusive memorial is for a girl who
suffered a fatal accident when the steep road was being built. One wonders
how many memorials are hidden or forgotten in fields or along country lanes.

monument and statue

LLANSANNAN   SH 933658

*The monument commands a central position
in the village.*

This impressive bronze statue of a girl
in Welsh dress is annually adorned
with fresh daffodils. The monument
is in memory of five writers, natives
of Llansannan: Tudor Aled; William
Salesbury (New Testament translator);
Henry Rees (said to be "one of the
greatest preachers and saintly men
in Wales"); Gwilym Hiraethog (William
Rees' nom de plume – brother of Henry),
"preacher, lecturer, journalist, reformer,
poet, evangelist and hymn writer"; and
Iorwerth Glanaled.

Monument
& Statue

all at sea

ABERGELE   SH 945776

You can find this tombstone in the churchyard at St. Michael's.

St. Michael's is in the centre of the town, half a mile due south of the beach. The inscription on the stone reads:

HERE LIETH
IN ST. MICHAEL'S CHURCHYARD
A MAN WHO HAD HIS DWELLING
THREE MILES TO THE NORTH

Was this a mistake? Did, perhaps, the man live along the coast to the west or have a houseboat in the midst of the shipping lines to Liverpool?

Memorial Stone

hallelujah obelisk

MOLD SJ 222647
For access, apply at
Rhual, across the
road from the site.

In 1736 Nehemiah
Griffith of Rhual
erected this obelisk.
Its Latin inscription
commemorates the
victory of the Britons
(Welsh) over the
Saxons and Picts
during the early
fifth century.

The battle was said
to have taken
place in this field
'Maes Garmon'.

After the victory
the Christian Britons,
including the saints
Germanus and Lupus,
shouted,
"Hallelujah".

Obelisk

The memorial was also a drinking fountain.

war memorial

FRONCYSYLLTE   SJ 274412

This roadside memorial is on the A5.

Travellers pass this monument at Froncysyllte without a glance, but on closer inspection the bluish terracotta memorial, for two privates from the Welch regiments, is a reminder of the typical causes of death amongst British soldiers sent to South Africa at the turn of the 20th century to fight in the Second Boer War. Whilst one of these soldiers died in battle the other suffered dysentery.

British expansion had created many of the problems that led to the war. The official adoption of the English language in 1823, closely followed by the emancipation of slaves in 1833, left the independently-minded Dutch Calvinists (Boers) feeling threatened. They saw themselves as the 'chosen people of God' and felt free to use the 'inferior' races of Africa as a source of free labour. After gold and diamonds were discovered in the Transvaal (a Dutch state under the British Queen Victoria since the First Boer War of 1880/1) Cecil Rhodes, the Premier of Cape Colony, backed an armed incursion (the Jameson Raid of 1895) which failed, leaving even the Prime Minister of Britain linked to the scandal.

The British had forces of only 25,000 at the start of the war in 1889 and suffered heavy losses. General Roberts with General Kitchener (who had recently retaken Khartoum) as Chief of Staff, took over supreme command in 1900 and appeared to vanquish the regular Boer units within six weeks, formally annexing the Transvaal in September 1900. The Boers adopted guerilla tactics and delayed the end of the war for another year and a half. By the peace treaty of 1902 over 30,000 Boer farms and villages had been destroyed by the British scorched earth policy. One hundred and twenty thousand Boers, mainly women and children, were incarcerated in concentration camps (the first in history) with 28,000 dying of disease including 4,000 women and 16,000 children. Britain had increased its forces and had 300,000 troops against a quarter the number of Boers.

During the war, 22,000 British soldiers died, over 13,000 from disease (mostly enteric fever), whilst a further 31,000 were invalided home. At the famous seige of Mafeking, Colonel Baden-Powell starved hundreds of the local black population by requisitioning or buying all the food for his soldiers. Starving natives caught stealing food were shot. A letter by Baden-Powell, and his later testimony to the Royal Commission for the War contained a great deal of fabrication. Although the natives were not generally armed in the war, as he stated, the Baralong were regularly used as snipers and their cattle raids helped feed the British army. Five hundred armed natives played a large part in defeating the final Boer assault upon Mafeking.

After the war, as a gesture of conciliation, white farmers received nearly £2 million for repatriation in the Transvaal whilst a mere £16,000 was spent on the black population. A policy of Anglo-Dutch equality was gradually accepted. Unfortunately this eventually led to Afrikaner nationalist resurgence and the apartheid policies, dismantled only recently.

War....
Throughout the centuries
musicians, artists and writers
have portrayed this theme of
duality which humanity has
not integrated into its psyche.

war & peace
LEESWOOD   SJ254620
The black gate lodges are on the south side of the B5444.

When George Wynne made his fortune by mining lead on
Halkyn Mountain he attempted to emulate the rich
aristocracy. In around 1725 he built Leeswood Hall,
complete with formal gardens, dovecote, icehouse and an
impressive entrance through white gates (see CC1 p 125,
CC2 p 11).

and Peace.
Famous examples are Holst with
his Planets : Mars, the Bringer of
War; Venus, the Bringer of Peace ;
Picasso's two studies ; and Tolstoy's
'War and Peace'.

However, the lead veins on the mountain were soon exhausted
and he died, bereft of wealth, in 1798. In the early 19th century,
much of the hall was demolished or remodelled by the new
owners. A new drive was built and the two lodges from
the 'White Gates' were moved to a new entrance alongside
the 'Black Gates', where they can still be seen. Each lodge,
with its Doric columns, has a sculpture: one of war,
one of peace.

dovecote memorial

CEFN

Ty Mawr Country Park is open to visitors all year round.

From being one of the world's expansionist aggressors, Britain has now joined with other countries to establish a peaceful basis for world politics through the U.N. and other means. Today's armed forces are primarily used for peacekeeping duties, but there are still casualties.

Beside the dovecote is the magnificent arched viaduct, built in 1848, by Henry Robertson for the Great Western Railway.

Doves have often symbolised peace (although they too have been used in war, see CC1 p 53) so it is understandable that a memorial by public donation should be a dovecote. The Ty Mawr cote is in memory of Lieutenant Corporal Wayne J Edwards of the Royal Welch Fusiliers who was killed whilst on peacekeeping duties with the Cheshire Regiment in Bosnia on 13th January 1993.

Opposite: the dovecote memorial.

two bridges

CHIRK   SJ286372

Cross the aqueduct by towpath, parking off Castle Road or in Chirk Bank. Walk under it from Chirk Mill or Pont Faen.

Work on Chirk Aqueduct over the River Ceiriog started on June 17th 1796. The 21 metre high structure was completed five years later. Cast-iron plates were set in the bottom of the masonry channel to hold water. An iron trough was added later, after the success of the iron Pontcysyllte Aqueduct over the River Dee, a few miles to the north. The canal opened in 1802. William Jessop had been the Chief Engineer while Thomas Telford had been the General Agent, Surveyor, Engineering Architecture and Overlooker of the Works. It was fairly clear who had done the work, and Telford became the Chief Engineer and designed Pontcysyllte Aqueduct.

Henry Robertson later dwarfed the Chirk Aqueduct with his viaduct beside it. Built for the Great Western Railway, it ran 30 metres above the river and was finished in 1848. Robertson had studied under another master, Robert Stephenson.

high bridge
BONTUCHEL

There are two bridges in the village, both on public roads.

If you do not speak Welsh you may not have realised that the name of the village derives from pont (bridge) and uchel (high). It probably referred to the central bridge and not the one shown in the engraving of 1795.

According to the 'Clwyd Historian' magazine, the architect of the later bridge was Joseph Turner from Chester. Robert Simon, a mason from Llandyrnog, built it for £170 and gave a seven year guarantee. Unfortunately he had to be called back under the guarantee's terms to rebuild the battlements.

'Pont Ychel' engraving

uphill river

LLANGOLLEN

The River Dee runs from Dduallt in Snowdonia to the Irish Sea.

In legend the 'supernatural' waters of the Dee or Dyfrdwy are said to stay separate from the existing water in Bala Lake as they run down from Dduallt in Snowdonia.

However, at least two engravings show the river running uphill at Llangollen. The bridge, together with the ruin of Castell Dinas Brân, were common features for artists portraying North Wales. But engravers often worked away from the subject matter on the basis of sketches and also had to engrave pictures in reverse, resulting in strange prints. The engraver, Catherall, should perhaps have realised his error as he worked in nearby Chester.

Water does run uphill on most rivers when the incoming tide hits the outgoing current in the estuary and a wave known as a 'bore' is created. On the Dee this bore measures up to a metre high and runs up the canalised river towards Chester. Much to his surprise, Mr James Bentley, who, in his retirement, canoed downhill from Bala, hit the bore on the Dee in darkness, but being forewarned by the noise of the wave, managed to turn his canoe and was washed, safely, into the shallows.

Engraving of Llangollen by T. Catherall

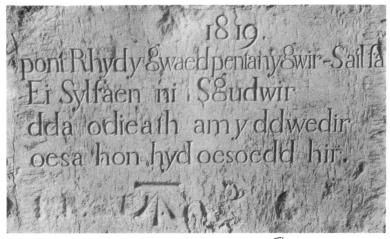

The poem

poem bridge
RHEWL   SJ 106604

The Ruthin - Denbigh road crosses the bridge

A Welsh poem in the 'Englyn' style, with four lines rhyming and an addition to the first line, is transcribed on this bridge of 1819. The translation has been slightly altered to keep the rhyme.

Blood ford bridge, truth mantle making — On bedrock
Its foundations withstand shaking
so well it will be waiting
for generations waking.

The bridge

pont faen
CHIRK

SJ280371

Most of Ogilby's roads are still on public highways but some of these highways are now just footpaths.

When William Day decided to trace the course of a 17th century highway from Chester to Cardiff he reached Pont Faen and decided that the 'cosmographer to the King', John Ogilby, had made a mistake nearly three centuries before. "The river seems to have been marked where the road is and vice-versa", claimed Day, " the road 'To Llangollen' the one north of the river" and not on the south as on Ogilby's map. Following this assumption Day then had to make a circuitous route southwest to Selattyn in Shropshire, entering the village by the western (instead of the obvious northern) entrance to make his theory fit.

Nearly two decades later the author of this book found his article in 'Transactions of the Shropshire Archaeology Society, Volume 60'. By reassuming that Ogilby had been right after all, and after a series of fortuitous discoveries, the author maintains that Ogilby's map was accurate. After realising that the toll road on the north bank of the river was only built in 1862, two centuries after Ogilby, the author found that the other road on the north bank shown 'To Oswastree' (Oswestry) ran from Chirk through the riverside meadow to Pont Faen. In the Quarter Sessions of July 1863, the owner of the meadow had this road closed as being 'no longer needed for public use' due to the new road.

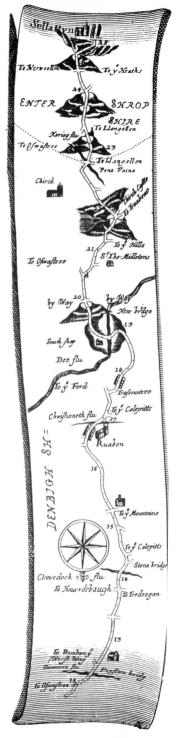

Another look at the roads south of the Ceiriog led to the conclusion that the southwestern road was the only route to Llangollen from here in the 17th century and followed the road and maybe what is now a footpath (part of the Maelor Way) to Bronygarth before crossing to the northern bank. The main highway to Cardiff can now be shown to go directly south to Weston Rhyn and then follow the (former Roman) road to Selattyn entering the village by the obvious northern entrance.

Finally, while reassessing the northern route which seemed to sweep towards Chirk Castle, the author found the ancient highway, a hollow way now swallowed up in the castle parkland. No record of its legal diversion has been found, although a road runs along the parkland boundary (Day thought it the 17th century one) and it is assumed that this was the replacement.

Left: Part of Ogilby's Chester to Cardiff road of 1675. The author's notes and up-to-date maps have been deposited at Shropshire Record Office, open to the public by appointment.

Right: Ogilby's road can be seen as a hollow way crossing the parkland at the first bend of the entrance drive and also crossing the permissive summer path from Ty'n-y-cil. Chirk Castle grounds are closed in winter.

Beneath the road is a hollow walkway in the 'box-girder' used
for maintenance.

viaduct

CHIRK   SJ300373

Go over the bridge by car or bike but pedestrians are prohibited. A footpath goes underneath.

Standing under the Ceiriog Viaduct, it is difficult not to be impressed by its grandeur.
This road bridge for the A5 (Chirk Bypass) designed by Travers, Morgan and Partners,
consists of a 470 metre long 'constant depth cellular pre-stressed concrete box
girder' which was cast in 32 segments on the south bank of the valley to form
a continuous section. This was then launched across the eight piers, and
temporary steel ones, at a rate of 15 metres a week during 1990. It is the
longest bridge of its type in Britain and stands 30 metres above the River
Ceiriog.

A pedestrian ban over the Ceiriog and Dee viaducts was enforced by the Welsh Office
who stated to consultees that no pavements had been provided on the bridges.
The Ramblers pointed out that there were, in fact, pavements in place. In true
bureaucratic style the Welsh Office proceeded with the ban anyway.

topiary

PONTBLYDDYN   SJ 277604

The hedge is at the main crossroads in the village.

The name 'PONTBLYDDYN' formed out of a hawthorn hedge was once famous in Clwyd. But in 1989 the hedge and its topiary name were destroyed. A lorry carrying clay crashed into the front garden when the driver swerved to avoid two old ladies in a car that had turned out of the Corwen road onto the A541. The current owner of the cottage, Albert Jones, planted a fast-growing Chinese honeysuckle hedge in 1993. The name of the village is to be famous once more.

The metal form for the growing hedge

Holt Bridge is on the site of a ferry crossing recorded in 1315.

holt or farndon bridge

HOLT   SJ412545

The bridge crosses the River Dee to Farndon in England.

Known by those who live in England as Farndon Bridge and those in Wales as Holt Bridge, it is recorded by Hubbard in 'Buildings of Wales' as being 15th or 16th century with eight arches. However, Pennant recorded it with ten in 1754 and stated that a 1354 date stone was present 'until recently'. Hubbard points out that the third segment from the Welsh side marks the site of a defensive tower.

Although it may have been restored or rebuilt, there was a bridge in the 14th century that had a tower. Records show that at the County Court of Chester on 12th September 1368, 'The jury presented that John, earl of Warenne, late Lord of Bromfeld, had constructed a bridge across the River Dee (during 1338) between Farndon and le Holt, half of which is built upon the land of Cheshire, and upon that bridge is a fortified gateway. The channel of the Dee has been shifted away from the Cheshire side by the officers of the earl of Arundell, lord of Bromfeld under Sir Robert de Astmede (receiver), by means of the night removal of great stones under the bridge to the disherion of the earl of Chester and the prejudice of his lordship'. Moreover they extorted daily toll from workmen crossing 'against the state of the said earl of Chester and the dignity of the sword of Chester. For example, Henry, son of Roger Pot de le Holt took a halfpenny from Richard le Rymour at Farndon'. 'Also a large number of felons are given shelter in the town of Holt...and frequently set up ambushes to rob the Cheshire people and hunt them, and they are given shelter by the Earl of Arundell and his officials'.

In 1627 a survey showed, "Upon the West parte of the Mannor over the River of Dee standeth a Bridge contayninge 10 arches which River divideth the Two Sheires, namely Cheshire and Denbye. And parteth the Mannor of Farndon and the Corporacion of Hoult. Upon the fifth Arch from Hoult standeth a Tower or Gatehouse of Fortificacion...(the text then describes Lady's Chapel in the tower)... Upon the other end of the fortificacion next unto the Mannor of Farndon is layd out in Masons Works a Lyon to the full passant. And like Lyon is upon the gates of Holt Castell. The County of Chester doth repair the bridge to the Lyon".

William Brereton, attacking Holt for the Parliamentarians stated, "for which end they had alsoe made a towre and drawbridge and strong gates upon the bridge soe as both they and wee conceived it verie difficult if not altogether ympossible to make way for our passage". Despite this he, Thomas Middleton and their forces took the bridge on 9th November 1643 when they cast 'some grenados amongst the Welshmen'.

Although it would seem that the bridge was originally built by the lord in Holt during 1338, by the 17th century repairs to the centre had been the responsibility of both shires. Now that two segments have gone and the remaining indication of the tower is on the third segment from the Welsh bank, five-eigths of the bridge would appear to be English. Should it still hold its historical name of Holt Bridge?

The third arch is now supported by a stone arch underneath.

chain bridge

LLANTYSILIO   SJ 200 433

Cross the Dee from Berwyn Station to the Llangollen Canal via this bridge.

Exuperius Pickering, an ironmaster who owned local collieries and lime kilns, built the first Chain Bridge in about 1817 to transport coal across the Dee. A local trade directory shows that he owned a forge at Pontcysyllte, so it is likely that he supplied the wrought-iron chains for the structure.

Henry Robertson, owner of the hotel and builder of the viaducts at Newbridge and Chirk (see pages 110&111), rebuilt the bridge in about 1870. This stood until 16th February 1928 when a severe flood caused fallen trees to form a dam across the upstream side of the bridge. Water built up until it flowed over the decking. Later that evening the bridge gave way. The main columns were swept away (the first two bridges were not completely suspension bridges) leaving only the chains and the bracing bars.

Sir Henry B Robertson, son of the previously-mentioned engineer, rebuilt the bridge the following year. Brymbo Steelworks supplied new fittings, although the chains were retained and lengthened. Whereas the original anchor point had been beside the river the new one was made on the other side of the canal. Two steel bars were set vertically into solid rock and capped with 2.5 metres of concrete. The bridge was opened in September 1929

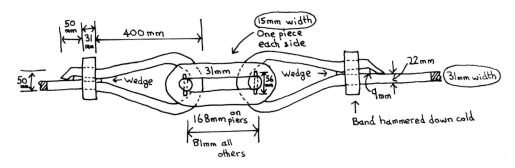

Left: Chain Bridge

Detail of Wrought-iron Joints (from Brymbo Steelworks Magazine 1929)

Ornamental Bridge

arched bridge
SOUGHTON   SJ247675

The fields are private but the bridge can be seen from
Soughton Hall.

In the middle of a field below Soughton Hall there is an
ornamental arched stone bridge. Now only used by
cattle and farm vehicles, in earlier times it would
have seen ladies in long dresses walking from the
hall on summer afternoons before tea or, perhaps,
on their way to a picnic.

Rear view of the hall with
one of the turrets.

turrets

SOUGHTON   SJ 247674

The hall is now a hotel.

The 18th century hall of Baroque design was remodelled in
a Spanish style then remodelled again by Douglas
according to Hubbard in 'The Buildings of Wales: Clwyd',
which gives a full description of the interior as well.
The unusual turrets or cupolas stand at the four
corners of the garden wall. They are more modern
than the house and were added by Sir Charles Barry
in the early 19th century after his Egyptian travels, thus
their Islamic style. They give a sense of mystery to the
otherwise neat symmetrical hall.

Cathedral

smallest cathedral

ST ASAPH   SJ039743

There is a car park at the rear of the cathedral.

With a total length of under 56 metres, naves and aisles
of 20 metres and the height of the tower less than 21 metres,
St Asaph (Llanelwy) Cathedral is the smallest in England and
Wales. It is also one of the oldest Christian sites in the
country, having been a monastery or 'clas' from the
mid-6th century. The cruciform stone building was started
in the 13th century with most of the work carried out in
the 14th. A tower was erected after completion of the
main building, but this had to be repaired after being
burnt by Owain Glyndŵr, and was also rebuilt in the
18th century. The cathedral contains the only medieval
canopied stalls in Wales, carved from oak with simple
rose decorations. (See also CC1 p114.)

Leicester's Church

unfinished church

DENBIGH SJ 053658

The church is private. It can be seen below Denbigh Castle where there is a themed display.

Robert Dudley, Earl of Leicester was a favourite of Queen Elizabeth I. So much so, that it was rumoured 'her Majesty visits him in his chamber day and night'. By 1561, coincidentally the year that Leicester's wife fell down the stairs and broke her neck, rumours were abroad that Elizabeth was to have his illegitimate child, or that she was 'a mother already', leaving several people 'shorter by a head' for making treasonable statements. (See also CC1 p 148.) The Queen's attachment to Leicester led him to marry in secret: Lady Sheffield in 1573, later denied, then Lettice Knollys in 1578. The Queen bestowed vast acres of land on Leicester. As Lord of Denbigh, and an extreme protestant or Puritan, he founded the church at Denbigh, also in 1578. He may have intended to transfer the bishopric from St Asaph but work was abandoned in 1584. For the next two years or so Leicester led an expedition into the Netherlands for the Queen. There he was proclaimed Governor General, much to the dislike of Elizabeth, who stated that she was 'utterly at squares with his childish dealing'. He died soon after, in 1588.

jacobite house

The owners of Berse Drelincourt hope to open the gardens to the public but meanwhile access is only by written permission.

When Bonnie Prince Charlie wrote to Lady Primerose of Berse Drelincourt under her pseudonym of "Miss Fines" and addressed her as "Dear Sister" it may have been a very different relationship he had in mind. The Jacobites in Wales were supported, in word if not in deed, by Sir Watkin Williams Wynn (III) of Ruabon who formed a Jacobite club, supporting the Stuart cause, as early as 1710. Scots pines are said to be planted at Jacobite houses to show the owners' allegiance: trees at Leeswood Hall were said to be an example of this.

Peter (Pierre) Drelincourt, Dean of Armagh, built Berse Drelincourt in 1715. The house had two tunnels, one presumably for escape purposes which emerged behind hedges, the other possibly used as a priest-hole. On the Dean's death in 1722 he bequeathed £700 for a charity school or orphanage. In 1739 his daughter married Viscount Primerose. The school was built in the grounds during 1747 and endowed by the Dean's widow, helped by public subscription, often from other Jacobite sympathisers. With two mistresses and 10 girls in the school, Lady Primerose reserved the right "to be the only visitor and the sole and absolute director of it in every respect". An historian, Dr King, noted that "Charles Edward actually appeared at one of Lady Primerose's parties in London, in 1750..." While running the school, Lady Primerose was in communication with the Stuart prince. A letter from Charles to "Miss Fines" in 1751 warned of people "concerned in your affairs" and another asked for his London home to be "furnished". It is said that in 1752 a certain lady bore a son to the young 'Chevalier St George' while staying on a French Estate. The child was taken to England and entered the navy in 1767 serving as Midshipman Douglas. (Charles had used the pseudonym Douglas while travelling incognito.)

After Lady Primerose died, Berse Drelincourt became the residence of the curate to Berse Drelincourt Church, built in 1742 for up to 150 Welsh speakers. The house, now a listed building, has suffered from years of neglect but the current owners are refurbishing it and replanting the formal gardens. As a modern addition they have designed a star-shaped Millenium Maze of about two thousand beech trees in the grounds.

Althrey Hall had to have 75% of its oak timbers replaced in an arduous piece by piece restoration over nine years.

medieval hall

BANGOR-ON-DEE   SJ 378441

Althrey Hall is open to the public by arrangement only. Contact Mr T. Smith (01978 780111).

Virtually abandoned to fate, Althrey Hall was in a ruinous condition when it was bought, in 1986, by Tom Smith. Originally a carpenter by trade he had become proficient at restoring timber-framed houses. His painstaking work at Althrey uncovered many clues to the building's history. Under the existing open hearth in the centre of the galleried great hall he found another hearth, and remains of another building under that.

Behind panelling in the main bedchamber two unique discoveries were made. A wall painting of the Tudor, Ellis ap Richard, and his wife Jane (Hanmer) is in remarkable condition apart from a little 16th century graffitti. Also hidden was an inflamatory pamphlet associating Jacobites with the Devil.

In the small chapel on the first floor a painted ceiling representing the Celestial City has a disguised entrance (not shown) into a priest hole in the attic.

wall painting

The church is open to the public on request - the keyholder's address is posted in the church porch.

In the spring of 1967 the Reverend Parry Jones discovered traces of a wall painting under several layers of white and colour wash in Llanynys Church. Part of what may have been a series of wall tapestries, this medieval depiction of St Christopher includes a halo in gold leaf around the Christ Child's head. The painting, believed to be from the first quarter of the 15th century, also depicts a windmill and fish, while the saint's staff is sprouting new life.

The legend of Christopher dates from the third century. He is said to have decided to serve the greatest prince in the world. After giving allegiance to a king who feared the Devil, he then worked for the Devil, only to find that the latter trembled at the sign of the cross (thus the windmill). Christopher decided to serve Christ but after failing to become a monk he took on the work of a ferryman carrying travellers over the river. After some time he heard the voice of a child asking to be carried across the river. Upon being called three times he lifted the child up and bore him through the waters. He was weighed down so much that he thought he would drown. When he reached the other bank the Child told him that he had carried the weight of all the world and its Creator as well. He then told Christopher to plant his staff beside his house where it would bear flowers and fruit.

Saint Christopher has become the patron saint of travellers.

Saint Christopher is depicted carrying the Christ Child across the river.

butterflies

GLYNDYFRDWY

The Original Butterfly Man Craft Workshops are on the A5. Phone 01490 430300.

When, in a walking guide to Glyndyfrdwy, the author wrote, 'these butterflies are becoming a local tradition', he had been caught by a simple but effective marketing ploy: Eos Griffiths had experienced problems selling his unique wall butterflies and finally, in desparation, fitted them free to houses along the tourist route asking only one consideration from their new owners — to tell anyone who asked, where they could be purchased.

His idea won attention from the public and the press. Mr Griffiths and his brightly painted butterflies were soon known worldwide, bringing orders addressed to 'The Butterfly Man, Near Llangollen.

Hibernating butterflies take cover in the shop.

Mainly unsuitable for modern farming methods, the steep-sided Welsh valleys are, perhaps, ideal for real butterflies. A recent study by Oxford University shows that organic farms, such as that belonging to the Prince of Wales at Highgrove in Gloucestershire, have twice as many common butterflies. For example gatekeeper and meadow brown are found in much greater numbers than those on farms using pesticides and herbicides.

Fire sign
BANGOR-ON-DEE

This original sign can be seen on a house beside the uphill bend of the A525 a mile southeast of the village.

" I don't know what he looked like, except a funeral, with the addition of a large Danish sun or star hanging round his neck by a blue ribbon, that had given him the appearance of being insured in some extraordinary Fire Office," so Dickens refers to Mr Wopsle dressed as Hamlet in 'Great Expectations'.

One of the Sun Firemarks may have been copied for the Llanerchrugog Estate, see front cover.

This copper sign shows the three leopards used as insignia for the Salop Fire Office. The animals were taken from the heraldry of Shropshire.

The sun that Dickens was alluding to was the firemark or firesign issued by the Sun Assurance Co., the first of its type in Britain. Other companies followed suite and the SALOP plate was issued by the Salop Fire Office which had formed in 1780 to cover loss and damage by fire in Shropshire and surrounding counties. The company, which operated from its director's house in Shrewsbury, later moved to the Corn Exchange, and then next to the Talbot Inn. The alleyway from the office to the fire engine garage became known as Fire Office Passage. The company employed firemen supplied with the Newsham type manual pump, ladders, hooks and buckets. Lead firemarks were issued until around 1826 and copper ones after that. For some time in the 1980s the Ironbridge Gorge Museum produced cast-iron reproductions.

The Fylfot on
the wall at
British Aerospace

Fylfot

BROUGHTON   SJ 345642

Access only to employees or by written permission from British Aerospace.

The resemblance of this small piece of terracotta to a swastika is obvious and, in fact, the dictionary states that 'fylfot' is a rare word for the symbol. The earliest known swastika is from Siberia, engraved under the wings of a flying bird carved from mammoth ivory. Other examples can be found in Iran (C18th BC) on a mother goddess figure, and Crete and Greece (C9th + C7th BC) on similar figures. A Trojan goddess figurine (C3rd BC) has a swastika carved in her pubic region. The British Museum have a set of Roman silverware with central swastikas.

The reason for its positioning at British Aerospace is more difficult to fathom. Perhaps it is because the fylfot was an ancient Asian peace symbol. This is the reason that the RAF's 273 Squadron adopted a cruciform fylfot (the Nazi swastika was canted and in reverse) for its squadron badge. Nicknamed the 'ghost squadron' it was originally founded during 1918 in Great Yarmouth for coastal reconnaissance then re-formed as part of Ceylon's fighter defence in 1939. The squadron badge has never been officially recognised by the Ministry of Defence. It is likely that some of the planes for the 273 Squadron were built by deHavilland at Broughton. However, although the fylfot on the wall is in reverse to the Nazi swastika, it is canted. So the reason for its existence is still a mystery.

dolos

COLWYN BAY   SH851791
The dolos is situated near the Tourist Information Office.

Is it a piece of modern art or a concrete monolith to celebrate the slicing in two of Colwyn Bay by the expressway? Five tons of concrete surround a mesh of interlaced iron to make this unusual object. Like a double-ended anchor it was built for a similar purpose: to prevent the drag of the tide. The word *dolos* comes from the Greek which translates as a 'bait for fish, or a cunning contrivance for deceiving or catching as in the net which Vulcan catches Mars'. The Latin 'dolus' had become to mean fraud, whereas the nearest Welsh word 'dolen' translates as loop, ring, or connection.

Dolos

21,999 doloi

LLANDDULAS   SH 895786

To find these doloi take the beach road at Llanddulas and walk along the shore towards Colwyn Bay.

An interlocking network of doloi is piled up along the shore at Llanddulas. They were placed there to protect the North Wales Coastal Trunk Road (A55T) from being washed into the sea. It was calculated that they would survive even the severest storms.

One advantage that was not foreseen by the contractors is that the doloi have become an ideal bed for seaweed. Thin strands of weed grow from the concrete surfaces and receive nourishment from the sea. Like all seaweeds (except the ones with bubbles) it is edible. For centuries this nutritious food, containing an abundance of amino acids, has been used as a Welsh breakfast recipe, laver bread, as well as a flavouring for cheese. Now it is often dried, imported from the Far east and sold as sheets of 'Nori'. The seaweed was once a common fertiliser for coastal farmers.

Laver hangs from the beak of the Laverbird or 'Liverbird' (a cormorant), used as a symbol of maritime importance, at the entrance to Liverpool dock. It is believed that the port was named after the seaweed.

Washed several times in clean water, some of the weed growing on these doloi was used for soups and stews by the author of this book. (Note that the water in the Irish Sea has been claimed to be both polluted and radioactive and even washing the seaweed may not make it suitable for consumption.)

The doloi, the author and the now eaten seaweed.

The giant building blocks in Wrexham

lego

WREXHAM   SJ 323501

Three bricks stand beside the A525 Ruthin Road.

Two eight stud Lego bricks of the same colour can be interlocked in 24 different ways: six bricks of the same colour give 102,981,500 combinations! With 1,720 different moulds for bricks, produced in a variety of colours, this creative toy has fired the imagination of millions of children worldwide.

Inspired by a British design from Kiddicraft, the first plastic forerunner of the Lego brick was produced in 1949. Ole Kirk Christiansen, a carpenter by trade, had started to produce toys in 1932 and, in 1934, named them Lego (from the Danish LEg GOdt = play well). By 1987 the LEGO product was accorded the title 'Toy of the Century.'

The virtually indestructible moulded plastic bricks have, in some cases, been handed down three generations and will, almost certainly, be handed down to a new generation in the 21st century.

The special 300 kilo bricks were installed outside the UK marketing headquarters in Wrexham during 1992.

Further reading: A universal concept of play, available from Lego.

County Hall (formerly Shire Hall) Mold. Was the architect influenced by the knobbled lego bricks? Unfortunately for the council, the building could not be split up like Lego and rebuilt in the four new county boroughs.

index

Compare the prehistoric 'Caergwrle Bowl' [left] (shown in more detail in CC1) with this prehistoric plate from Egypt [right]. The bowl is said, by archaeologists, to represent a boat with eyes, oars, waves and shields. The plate (which could also be described as a bowl) apparently shows the sky (with the sun rising and setting), the earth and the sea. Two triangles (possibly mountains, nets or pyramids) with this pattern can still be found over the main entrance to the Great Pyramid at Giza.

The dismantled chimney at Llanerch-y-mor Leadworks (see also CC1 p 66,67)

Half a church is better than none!
St Hilarys was built as a chapel for
Denbigh Castle. It can be found
near Leicester's unfinished church.

Eyton Manor Farm, more pretty than curious.
c 1633

other guides by gordon emery

CURIOUS CLWYD   £11-95*

Explore Clwyd's cabinet of curiosities — more than 150 in the first volume
of Curious Clwyd together with listings of dovecotes, ice houses and beeboles.

GUIDE TO THE MAELOR WAY   £5-95*

From Offa's Dyke Path to the Sandstone Trail, this guide gives detailed
directions, maps and points of interest for walkers or just armchair
readers.

FAMILY WALKS ON THE NORTH WALES COAST   £5-50*

Sixteen walks with 29 alternative lengths from 1mile to 10 miles. Explore
the glorious countryside close to the popular resorts. Museums, galleries
and theatres are also listed. Starting points from stations or bus stops.

FAMILY WALKS IN THE NORTH WALES BORDERLANDS   £5-50*

Sixteen circular walks with shortcuts cover the Vale of Llangollen and
the Clywedog Valley. With rainy day alternatives. Starting points can be
reached by public transport.

WALKS IN CLWYD   99p each *

Send a S.A.E for the current list of these booklets. Each contains an
interesting walk, a map and line drawings.

DAYWALKS: VALE OF LLANGOLLEN (co-author John Roberts)   £4-95 *

Thirty-five linked routes in the Vale and surrounding hills. Choose your own
distance.   *prices correct 1996, liable to change.

In bookshops and information offices, Northeast Wales and Chester.